TOWARDS A THEORY OF KNOWLEDGE

TOWARDS A THEORY OF KNOWLEDGE

DR. DAYANIDHI SATAPATHY

DISCOVERY PUBLISHING HOUSE
NEW DELHI-110002

First Edition-1991

Reprinted-2013

ISBN 81-7141-115-0

Published by

DISCOVERY PUBLISHING HOUSE PVT. LTD.

4383/4B, Ansari Road, Darya Ganj

New Delhi-110 002 (India)

Phone: +91-11-23279245, 43596064-65

Fax: +91-11-23253475

E-mail: discoverypublishinghouse@gmail.com

sales@discoverypublishinggroup.com

parul.wasan@gmail.com

web: www.discoverypublishinggroup.com

Printed at:

Dynamic Printers

Delhi

Acknowledgements

In undertaking this study I am especially indebted to Dr. R. Sundara Rajan, Professor, Department of Philosophy, University of Poona, Pune, who has guided me throughout my study. It is due to his valuable guidance from time to time. I have been able to complete the work within the stipulated time.

I must also thank University Grants Commission, New Delhi, for having provided me a fellowship under the Faculty Improvement Programme, the authorities of University of Poona, Pune, the Principal and the Management of the D. A. V. College, Koraput, Orissa, and the D. P. I. (Higher Education), Orissa, for granting me, enobbling circumstances, physical and intellutual, for three years, free from regular academic duties in which I could undertake to finish this study.

I would fail in my duty if I do not express my heartfelt feelings of gratitude to my wife, whose continuous co-operation and encouragement was a source of inspriation to complete this work.

DAYANIDHI SATAPATHY

Preface

The present studies take the form of historical and systematic investigations of the problem of innateness. A very misleading and superficial view takes the problem of innate ideas to be merely of antiquarian interest as it is claimed that the controversy had been onced and for all settled by the outcome of the debate between Locke and Descartes. According to this view, the problem of innate ideas is purely of historical interest and has no systematic relevance for our present philosophical investigations. But as I attempt to show in these studies, the conventional opinion on this matter is inaccurate and misleading on both historical and systematic grounds. In the historical aspect, as I show in an appendix (Appendix B) on Locke-Descartes debate, the controversy is far more complex than it is made out, and also, more importantly, it is far from being clear and settled that Locke had successfully shown the untenability of the doctrine in the form that Descartes had actually held. In fact, it was the realisation of the complexity of the debate, that motivated me to study the historical development of the problem from Plato to Modern times. But when I began to undertake such historical studies, I also began to realise that the doctrine of innateness in fact, is the foundation question of epistemology, for in intention, if not in actual formulation, the question at issue here is the non-empirical conditions of the possibility of experience and knowledge. I believe that this is the basic issue which the doctrine of innateness has attempted to tackle and hence I consider the debate over the concept of innateness to be one of those ultimate and crucial debates which shape and structure the development of not merely epistemological reflections, but of philosophical investigation itself. I try to show that there is an underlining systematic continuity which persists in spite of contextual differences; I call the continuity, a continuity of function, for I argue that in all the various contexts in which the doctrine had been formulated, the basic philosophical question involved is the conditions of the possibility of experience and knowledge and I try to show how this *invariant question* has received different *contextually relative* formulations at different stages in the development of doctrine, and now this question supplies the thread of continuity in all these debates. This perspective on the concept of innateness brings out two important aspects of the problem, which in fact, serve as two basic motivations of these studies: (1) From the point of view of the basic logic of epistemological enquiry, the fundamental problem is the question about the conditions of the possibility of the knowledge; (2) From the point of the view of history of philosophical ideas, the career of the doctrine of innateness suggests that the issue has undergone a series of contextual variations till it receives a "transcendental" formulation in the critical philosophy of Kant. Accordingly, I believe that both from the systematic and historical points of view, the problem of innateness is likely to be a rich source of fresh and suggestive illumination.

In the case of a complex philosophical theme like that of the conditions of possibility of experience, I believe that one of the most useful ways of clarifying the nature of the fundamental issues at stake, is a genetic-analytical investigation which would bring out the development of the problem and reveal the process of its refinement and precise formulation. Very frequently in philosophical investigations, such historical studies give us new perspectives on the systematic question at stake, especially so in the case of a problem like that of innate knowledge where there is a *rich tradition of debate* from the Platonic period onwards. Accordingly Part 1 of the present studies attempt this kind of historical and genetic clarification. In these historical chapters I have selectively focused on certain major stages in the development of the problem, namely, the Platonic doctrine, the Medieval speculations of Augustine, Bonaventure, and St. Thomas Aquinas, the Renaissance discussions in the philosophy of nature and man, the Cartesian and Empiricist debate and the Copernican transformation of the problem brought about by Kant.

On the basis of the preceding historical discussion of the problem, in Part 2, I formulate the new perspective on the concept of innateness, which I call "Towards a Meta-theory of innateness". This reformulations is inspired by the Kantian paradigm of a transcendental argument; this reformulation, I argue, helps us to avoid the earlier confusions and controversies, when the question is posed on the first-order level, as to what is innate. This first-order formulation I show leads us to ontological, theological or psychological questions, whereas the transcendental formulation operates on the second-order level, as a meta-question about the 'critical' meaning of innateness. But apart from giving us a new *form* to the question, it also gives us a clue to the possibility of developing a Kantian or "critical" conception of innateness: as I argue in detail in the chapter on Kant, with the transcendental turn, the innate element in knowing has to be seen in terms of the *a priori synthesis* which is the ground of the possibility of knowledge. The concept of innateness now has a purely epistemic significance as standing for the synthetic activity of the mind which is the very pre-supposition and ground of knowledge and experience. I try to show how this meta-level formulation of the question brings out the methodological and epistemological intentions of the doctrine. I also try to show how this conception gets further support and precision in terms of three important Post-Kantian philosophical developments, Phenomenology, Genetic-Epistemology and Analytic philosophy. I try to show how these developments bear upon different aspects of the transcendental mode of argument and how they give precision and a more exact form to the basic ideas of the Kantian critique. These contemperory movements of thought, therefore, bring out the relevance of Kant for our present philosophical concerns, but they also sugguest possibilities of further development.

Although historical discussions form an important and integral part of the structure of my research studies, yet I have been selective in such discussions; my intention is not to provide an exhaustive and narratively complete account, I am conscious that I have not provided a discussion of the history of the problem in all its details and complexities. Even within the limits of a particular thinker or period, I do not aim to cover all aspects of the particular treatment of the problem. For example, with reference to Plato, I concentrate on only on the *Meno*, the *Phaedo* and the *Theaetetus*. Similarly while dealing with the Medieval period, I concentrate on only Augustine, Bonaventure and Aquinas. But perhaps the most important historical limitation is to be seen in terms of its culmination in the Kantian tradition of critical philosophy. These limitations and selectivities are due to the basic intention of the project, namely, to bring out 'the transcendental' character of the debate. I wish to focus on the 'critical' meaning of the doctrine as concerned with the grounds of the possibility of knowledge and naturally, therefore, I have concentrated only on those aspects of the historical development of the doctrine which bear upon this methodological and epistemological aspects of the problem. The same intention also explains why I have not considered certain contemperory discussions of the problem, such as that of Noam Chomsky. These developments no dobut, have great importance and interest on their own but as I try to show in the chapter called "Towards a Meta-theory of Innateness", my primary concern is with the transcendental transformation of the meaning of innateness brought about by Kant's critical philosophy. Given this second-order interest and pre-occupation, I found that the Kantian tradition gives us a natural terminus.

But by this I do not certainly wish to imply or suggest that there are no more problems left or questions yet to be raised and answered. On the contrary; I am only too well aware of the fact that there are so many more clarifications needed: for example, the problem of psychologism, of the status of the transcendental subject etc. are a few of the issues which require prolonged and continued study. I try to sketch a possible way of dealing with some of these questions, but I am aware that they demand a more extensive treatment. I hope to return to them in my future philosophical researches.

D. N. S.

Contents

PART I

Preparation for a Meta-Theory of Innateness

1

Innateness and Recollection in Plato

(i) Theory of Recollection

My central concern in this chapter would be an examination of three Platonic doctrines, *Theory of Recollection*; *Pre-existence of Soul*; *Theory of Forms* and their inter-relationship. While doing so my purpose would be to study the notion of innate-idea, its role in the formation of knowledge, which is inherent in the above doctrines and to see how Plato successfully established the recollection of non-sensible *Forms* which are innately there in the human mind as necessary for acquisition of knowledge.

Plato introduced the theory of recollection as a solution to the problem inherent in Socretic method for the attainment of knowledge, which was first presented in the *Meno* (80-6), subsequently confirmed in the *Phaedo* (72-7). There is also a reference to this problem in the *Phaedrus* (247-5) which would not be important for our discussion.

The theory of recollection is a process of gaining knowledge in this life by recollecting what the soul knew prior to the present life. Thus it is a theory which advocates that knowledge is a priori in the sense that its source is independent of experience. The nature of this theory is made clear in the course of the dialogue between Socrates and a slave-boy in the *Meno*. An ignorant slave is chosen for the purpose who had no previous knowledge of geometry, but recognised the difference between indubitabily true or false proposition brought to his notice for the first time. This recognition, without the previous knowledge of geometry, implies that the truth was a possession of the soul incarnated in human forms. It also implies that the truth is still in the soul; otherwise there would be no possibility of eliciting it in this life. Thus Plato's claim is that all knowledge is a *priori*.[1]

Socrates says that the Soul is immortal and undergoes reincarnation. That soul has witnessed everything here and in *Hades*. This conception of immortality of soul would become clearer when an account of the *Phaedo* would be given. Socrates even claimed that it is not surprising to say that the soul should able to recollect things that a knew before. Therefore he answers Meno's objections by showing that it is possible to have innate or latent knowledge, which may arise into our consciousness by association of ideas.

The main point is that since all learning is recollection, it may lead to an infinite regress, so theory of recollection does imply some conception of transcendent reality. So Socrates, infact assumes that the soul would have been in a state of knowledge for all time, even before birth. The slave in the *Meno* possessed the knowledge because he had already learnt it. Thus "the theory of *Anamnesis* logically involves belief in transcendent forms."[2]

Socrates illustrates this conception of latent or innate knowledge by putting geometrical questions to the slave-boy of the *Meno*. Putting questions by way of dialogue the expected answers were coming out, which ultimately convinced Meno to accept that the slave must have been in possession of those opinions before his birth, simply those opinions have been *stirred up* in him through dialogues of mathematics, which are true independently of the experience of this life altogether. That needs a systematic questioning to elicit the recognition. It follows that what one does not *know*—that is, remember—one should endeavour to recollect. And this recovery of knowledge is known precisely as recollection. Therefore to Plato, it seems, a priori knowledge could not be transmitted through word of mouth or produced by sensible images alone, it is only to be recollected by questioning suitably.

In this recollection which is a process, there is no question of sudden jump from ignorance to knowledge. That process involves three stages. The *first stage* prepares the way for the eliciting of the correct reply not only by eliminating false opinions and creating a desire to replace them by true ones, but also by offering positive hints or evidence which can be used in the search. The *second stage* is the "stirring up" of innate or latent true opinions and the *final one* is the conversion of this into knowledge.

Theory of Recollection in the Phaedo

The theory of recollection is presented in the *Meno* only as a possible interpretation of learning, the *Phaedo* provides a proof of the theory, which is treated as reliable. This theory makes clear that there is a possible answer to the *sophistic* question how can we discover anything which we do not know. The suggestion is, if the *Orphic doctrine of the immortality* and *transmigration of the soul* is correct, then the soul would be hold everything in this world and the next. In the *Meno* it seems that Plato was struggling to evolve a theory according to which the *objects* or *forms*, that we recollect have a real, supra-sensible, substantial existence, therefore in the *Phaedo* we are introduced to the doctrine of the *Forms.*

First in the *Phaedo*, inquiry begins in the direction of soul's search for ultimate truth. Such as 'the just itself', the 'beautiful', the 'good', 'tallness', 'strength', etc., as real nature of everything. These entities are declared to beyond the apprehension of bodily senses. As to a proof of the existence of these we come to the theory of recollection. Further we can justify the doctrine like—we know what we mean by perfect equality, although we have never in this world seen two things that everyone would agree to perfectly equal. Then at what time did we acquire this type of knowledge ? This clearly implies it is not in this life, but it must have been before we born. We must have lost this knowledge at birth and we can be reminded of these perfect entities, which we call by theory of recollection.

Thus Plato's theory of recollection became the basis of an argument for the existence of *Forms,* which in turn are made the grounds of the final proof of the soul's immortality.

The first proof of immortality may be stated as below—the term 'dead' implies logically that previously it was 'living' and vice-versa. Similarly we can pass from one state to its opposite state, such as 'smaller', to the 'larger', it could never have been larger unless it had gone through a similar process in the opposite direction.[3] Similarly there must be an opposite process of 'dying' which comes from 'living', this suggests that our soul must exist somewhere after our death waiting to be born again. If this reciprocal process would not have been there then sooner or later there would be no question of more births because the stock of souls would be exhausted.[4]

The above argument never presupposes that our souls after death retain intelligence, this part of the proof depends upon the theory of recollection. In this life we have the knowledge of various kinds of perfection, such as perfect equality, although we never have any perception of it, therefore this knowledge must have resulted from latent knowledge which was innately there in the human mind acquired before birth, of which we are simply reminded here through sense-perception. This implies that our souls existed before birth and had intelligence.

To the above thesis a number of objections may be raised because Plato has applied the principles of physical phenomena to an entity which it is claimed to be immortal, to which ordinary physical laws may not confirm. It is also possible that the stock of soul is unlimited or even that souls can be created out of nothing. Plato undoubtedly believed, that the soul could not be created out of nothing, rather he was attempted to demonstrate soul's immortality on mechanistic principles, as a second best, the certain method of attaining truth being by way of the discussion of Forms.

If Plato did not believe the above proof to be convincing, then why did he present it ? In considering the theory of forms, Plato accepted a contemporary notion that if a thing exists at all, it must have substantial existence independent of our minds. We have also seen that he believed that a soul could not be created out of nothihg. The main intention of Plato in demonstrating the immortality of soul by means of mechanistic principles is to convince those who were impressed only by mechanistic arguments, that even on their premises the immortality of soul could plausibly be defended. And this is the only reason why Plato devised his new theory of Forms.

Then it followed by argument from 'affinity', which stands as follows : Out of two components of Man, the body seems to have an affinity with the visible world of changing physical phenomena while the soul has an affinity with the invisible world of things unchanging and divine. The Soul belongs to the class of things that are invariable, constant and incomposite so that it is unchanging and everlasting. If even the body could remain for a considerable time after death, the soul must be everlasting. This argument does not constitute a final proof of the soul's immortality. But Simmias and Cebes[5] admit that, the soul is stronger and live longer than the body but cannot accept that it lasts for ever. But the argument from affinity is an argument of probability.

In spite of all arguments, Simmias and Cebes could not be convinced regarding the immortality of soul, which is the important point in the present context. Plato, hence came up with his *theory of forms* to the rescue of Socrates. Platonic Forms appear in a form of cause; everything that an object is or does will be the result of its participation in some *Form of Forms*. No Form or Form-Copy can ever reflect or taken upon itself the nature of its opposite, if it has one. For example, at the approach of heat, snow melts or as Plato would say the snow perishes or withdraws and something is generated, because logically no Form accepts its opposite. Similarly the soul which brings life cannot admit its opposite death.

In order to make the above logical point regarding participation more clear, Vlastos argument of 'aitia' would be of worth mention. We will consider only one meaning of 'aitia' that is 'cause' over-looking others in the present context.[6]

The formula stands as follows:

"Each of the Forms exists and it is in virtue of participating in them that other things are named after them." (102A 10-B2)

This formula has three sets of items and the relation of participation.

1. Forms are immutable incorporeal, divine, they cannot be known by sense experience, but only by recollection.

2. The individual persons and objects of ordinary experience, designated by proper names and definite descriptions.

3. The immanent characters of these individual, designated by adjectives, obstract nouns and common nouns. The very same words also name Forms, which particularly advocates the immanent and transcendent nature of Forms.

Using symbols for Schematic reference, the formula stands as below : F, G as character variables, F_1G_1 as Form variables, a, b, c, for names of individual and 'x' as a variable whose values are names of individuals. What the formula advocates is this : For any character 'F', of any individual, 'x', there exists a *homonymous* Form F_1. 'x' is 'F', if and only if 'x' participates in F_1. "Participation" here implies a one-way relation of ontological dependence between temporal things and external Forms which is very fundamental a tenet of Plato's philosophy.

Then the problem arises why is x F ? Let us consider in this connection about 'ignorant' and 'clever' 'aitia'. In connection with ignorant 'aitia', it is uniformative rather tautological where Socrates discusses examples like ten being more than eight etc. Rather from our point of view the 'clever aitia', which are informative, need to be discussed as an answer to the question why is x F ?

According to 'clever aitia', the formula stands as follows: 'x' is 'F' because it participates in G_1 and G_1 entails F_1, or more elaborately, x is F because, being G, it must participate in G_1, and since G_1 entails F_1, x must also participate in F_1, and hence x must be F. In application of the above formula we may examine the relation in terms of physical, biological and other examples of Form G_1 entailing F_1, such as—Fire-heart, snow-cold, fever-sickness, soul-life, etc.

By such considerations we may prove the immortality of soul. As the soul participates in life and life entails immortality, therefore, soul is immortal. Vlastos makes it clear that Plato does not spell out any such formula, but an examination of his text goes to suggest with the above view.

Hence Plato concluded that if we can accept that there is such a thing known as soul, and that it gives us life, which is its essential attribute, the above arguments would appear to be incontrovertible.

Finally we may note that Plato's claim that the soul has intelligence left after death is based not on these arguments, but on his doctrine of the recollection of Forms. The theory of recollection is extremely important, because it is concerned with the individual soul, it suggests the survival of intelligence and above all it necessitates the existence of perfect realities, which are later called *Forms* in an unseen world.

From the discussion of the *Phaedo*, we may conclude that, Plato insists in his *theory of Forms*, and these Forms of the *Phaedo* are to be recollected, which are innately there in the human mind in order to have any form of knowledge. This philosophical stand point would be more clear, if we would proceed to the *Theaetetus.*

(ii) Critique of Perception in the Theaetetus

The discussion regarding the theory of recollection in the *Meno* and *Phaedo*, would not be final unless we also consider the *Theaetetus*, where Plato discusses elaborately *Socratic definition of knowledge.*

In the first part of the *Theaetetus* there is no direct presentation of Plato's view; rather we have an examination of the assumption that "knowledge is perception." This implies acceptance of the thesis of *Protagoras* that "Man is the measure of all things", From this it follows that perception is infallible, which is assumed in the claim that knowledge is perception. Plato argues that Protagoras' thesis rests in turn on thesis that all things are in motion and perpetually changing.

In what way then does the *Heraclitian* flux doctrine supports the claim that knowledge is perception ? According to Plato the infallibility of perception can be shown to be a consequence of the doctrine that all things are in flux. For if everything is in flux, then it will follow that all percepts are the results of an interaction between constantly changing sense-organs and a constantly changing environment. But ultimately Plato holds that these two doctrines are inconsistent If everything is in flux, then nothing is ever the same; if nothing is ever the same, then no two percepts are ever the same, if no two percepts are ever the same, then the percepts of one individual are always different from others and hence private and peculiar to the individual.

Plato develops this point, that 'being in flux', is incompatible with 'being determinate', to hold that what is perpetually changing cannot be knowledge. Thus the claim, that knowledge is perception is disproved, in so far as it is based on the view that all things are in flux. Theaetetus shows that Plato accepts that all sensibles are in flux and hence can argue that if knowledge is to be possible, it is necessary to assume the existence of some determinate non-sensible realities. His argument is that no knowledge is derived exclusively from perception. Thus to take the example of 'This is yellow' or 'This is a stone'' Plato would say that while 'yellow' and 'stone' are perceptible characteristics, the simple judgement 'this is yellow' or this is stone' includes the application of 'being' which is apprehended by the mind independent of perception.

However Plato describes the apprehension, which is done independently of perception is known as *doxa,* whose meaning may either be judgement or belief. But Norman Gulley has accepted here the meaning of *doxa as belief.*[7] Here Plato proposed a definition of knowledge in the form of 'true doxa with an account' but adding such 'an account' yields only a trival distinction, because in order to give 'an account', we have to apply the method of analysis. He suggests 'an account' is possible only of what is complex but no account can be given, which cannot be analysed into simpler components, that ranks as absolute simples. To Plato the complexes are knowable and simples are unknowable. Hence no other account is possible for providing knowledge of particulars, since the claim of perception to provide knowledge has already been dismissed, Plato is ready to conclude that the sensible particular is unknowable. It is not amenable to the systematically rational account which is possible only for the Form. In this way, the difficulties of Theaetetus lead Plato to a re-affirmation of the reality of the Forms as objects of knowledge and superior to sensible particulars.

It is interesting to note what he says here and what he had said earlier about knowledge of Forms, specially the part played by perception. It is assumed in the *Republic* that the knowledge is of *Forms* and *Forms* only, that there is an inferior level of apprehension, which is not directed to Forms at all but exclusively to sensibles, which Plato calls as *doxa* and that perception has no contribution to make knowledge. In the *Phaedo*, in connection with the theory of recollection, Plato assumes that each Form has perceptable instances. If we compare the *Phaedo* and the *Republic* in these respects with the *Theaetetus*, it becomes clear that the *Theaetetus* is introducing a distinction, which was not there in the *Phaedo* and *Republic*. Rather the *Theaetetus* emphasizes that a full understanding of what is apprehensible by the mind itself is the result. Here Plato would at least grant that what is apprehended is a priori and it has the status of Form.

It is now clear from the *Theaetetus* that Forms are necessary rather than a sufficient condition for attainment of knowledge, but at the same time those Forms are to be recollected; otherwise it will not be resulted in knowledge. In other words, it is the knowledge which is to be recollected, which is innately there in the form of Forms in the human mind. Here the suggestion of Vlastos may be noted, that it is not knowledge which is innate, even 'latent' knowledge, but something else, apperently the true-opinion.[8] This statement of Vlastos creates quite a confusion even within the dialogues of Plato. The 'true-opinion' which is innate according to Vlastos, is surprisingly very right, because Plato identified even 'true-opinion' as knowledge in the *Meno*. If we consider the *Meno* only, the opinion of Vlastos is quite similar to that of Plato, but if we extend this towards other dialogues of Plato, we find, ultimately a contradiction in Plato, because no where except the *Meno*, does Plato identify true-opinion with knowledge. In the *Timaeus*, Plato assumes an absolute distinction between knowledge and belief. He advocates that the knowledge is of Forms and belief is regarding sensible, therefore there is no possibility of identification.

We may now consider here the learning principle of Socrates. His dialogues demonstrate that the learning for acquisition of knowledge is possible provided one is free from all types of false belief and prejudice. In order to achieve the above state, Socrates has to put suitable questions to the Slave-boy, so that from the beginning he has to clear himself from all types of false opinion that he has got. This type of learning pre-supposes that Socrates was insisting upon *negative type of epistemology*, which advocates that the knowledge is to be recollected, which is already there innately in the human mind, not a *positive epistemology of empiricism*. This negative epistemology, pre-supposes that the concepts and propositions are innately there in the human mind, only after recollection of those, knowledge is possible, so that Plato has given an *a priori* claim to that effect. But a possible objection can be raised here, because Plato does not distinguish concepts from propositions. Replying to this objection, Plato argued that inspite of important differences, there are also important similarities between the two, and particularly the differences are not relevant to the discussions here. Even Kant did not find differences between concept and propositions, rather he argued that one may talk of necessary connections between concepts and necessary links between propositions interchangeably. Thus the recollection thesis shows that there must be concepts and propositions given innately to the human mind in the form of *Forms* and those are to be recollected in order to have knowledge.

(iii) Mid-wifery as Philosophical Method

In addition to the above exposition of Plato's theory of recollection, some other relevant questions may arise, if we unravel it further. The theory of recollection which is discussed in the *Meno*, supposed to be an earlier dialogue of Plato,[9] may not be accepted as a fundamental doctrine. So that our above exposition may not be sound so far its doctrinal strength is concerned. Here the question may arise regarding the authenticity of the theory of recollection in the *Meno*. But if we compare this further with other fundamental and later dialogues of Plato, such as the *Theaetetus*,[10] we find the technique of Mid-wifery has got a sufficient relevance to the theory of recollection.

Let us first see the philosophical exposition of the concept 'Mid-wifery' as it has been suggested by Plato in the *Theaetetus*

(149A)—"... Like the mid-wife who is past child bearing, Scorates' function is not to pronuce his own ideas and impart them to others, but to deliver their minds of thoughts with which they are in labour, and then to test whether these thoughts are genuine children or mere phantoms."[11]

This suggests that the art of mid-wifery consists in eliciting from the pupil what he already has in him, this is possible provided the right answer is elicited from him in the right order. The argument of Socrates in this connection is that he already knew what they were and since he had not learnt them on earth, he must have learnt them before he was born. Therefore he argued learning is recollection in the *Meno*. In the *Meno*, Socrates explicitly makes the point that his argument shows that a mind must all times, whether before or after birth, have already learnt everything, therefore there never was a moment at which the learning occurred. It must be a timeless feature of the mind that to come to understand something is to elicit it from what is already in the mind.

This theory of recollection appeared in the *Theaetetus* in the form of the doctrine of mid-wifery, whose function is only to help a man who has an idea about something to bring that to birth. Because Socrates has the faith that if we have got any idea regarding anything, it is always possible that it is good one, and in that case he would play the role of an *intellectual midwife* to bring that to light and help him to get the idea clearly and state it distinctly.

In the *Meno* when Socrates asked to define Virtue, Meno made the same mistake as Theaetetus. There Meno's complaint was, Socrates does nothing but reduce others to perplexity; this complaint is here quoted by Socrates himself. Therefore F.M. Cornford rightly remarked—"At this point there follows in the *Theaetetus* the description of the art of midwifery, in the *Meno* the theory of *Anemnesis*—that all learning is the recovery of latent knowledge possessed by the immortal soul. One of the few valuable remarks of the Anonymous commentator is upon the equivalance of these two conceptions :

"Socrates calls himself a midwife because his method of teaching was of that kind ... for he prepared his pupils themselves to make statements about the subject by unfolding their natural ideas and articulating them, in accordance with doctrine that what is called learning is really recollection, and that every human soul has had a vision of reality, and needs, not to have a knowledge put into it, but to recollect'. There is some evidence that the historic Socrates professed the art of spiritual midwife; but Anamnesis appears first in the middle group of dialogues and provides the link between two Platonic doctrines : the eternal nature of the human soul and the 'separate' existence of Forms, the proper object of knowledge. The probable inference is that Anemnesis was a theory which squared the profession and practice of Socrates with Plato's discovery of the separately existing Forms and his conversion from Socratic agnosticism to belief in immortality."[12]

This technique of midwifery advocated by Socrates in the *Theaetetus* aims at a positive end, by means of destroying the habit of confounding a universal with its instances, and this is regarded as an essential preparation for the work of theory building. All these expositions of the art of midwifery now sufficiently justify its commitments to the theory of recollection, as to a proof of its doctrinal strength in order to accept our thesis that recollection is not only a discussion confined to the *Meno* but also extends to other fundamental doctrines of Platonic dialogues. Therefore it is remarked—"whether the argument seems sound to the moder readern or not, *Anemnesis* is accepted by all parties and later reaffirmed, nor is any doubt ever cast upon it in Plato's other works."[13]

Therefore we may conclude that the theory of recollection which aims at recollecting the latent ideas, has got its authentic relevance to the art of midwifery of the *Theaetetus*. The art of midwifery therefore suggested that the idea which is there innately in the human mind can only be elicited by playing the role of a midwife as Plato does to Theaetetus.

(iv) Socratic 'Elenchus'

The theory of recollection and its authentic relevance to the doctrine of midwifery has its further link with another outstanding method in Plato's earlier dialogues i.e., the Socratic 'Elenchus'.[14] "Elenchus in the wider sense means examining a person with regard to a statement he has made by putting to him questions calling for further statements, in the hope that they will determine the meaning and the truth value of his first statement. Most often the truth value expected is falsehood, and so 'elenchus' in the narrower sense is a form of cross examination or refutation."[15] If we explain it further in the light of the above we find that Elenchus changes an ignorant man from the state of falsely supposing that he knows to the state of recognising that he does not know. This is an important step for the construction of knowledge, because the recognition that we do not know arouses the desire to know and this supplies the motive that was lacking before. We should not suppose that Elenchus only instills knowledge, but it is an essential step to the removal of all bars to knowledge, which is naturally present in man. The aim of Elenchus is not to switch a man from an opinion that happens to be false to an opinion that happens to be true, rather the aim of Elenchus is to arouse men from their dogmatic slumbers into genuine intellectual curiosity.[16] This point we find explicitly mentioned by Socrates in the *Meno.* In the *Meno,* Plato presupposes curiosity as essential to the acquisition of knowledge and the Elenchus is the way to arouse curiosity. Elenchus is thus a method or technique of instilling intellectual knowledge in other persons. But this method or technique never increases knowledge rather it prepares a ground for knowledge.

Here a pertinent question may be raised as to the accepted interpretation of Plato's dialogue the *Meno*. In the *Meno,* it is stated, Plato accepted right opinion as knowledge, which has already been discussed, but now it seems evident from the technique of Elenchus which is present in the *Meno,* this view does not seem to be correct. Because notion the of Elenchus contains a germ of the Platonic conception of knowledge as absolutely distinct from opinion. The Elenchus does not directly give to a man any positive knowledge, but it gives to him for the first time the idea of real knowledge, without which he can never have any positive knowledge.[17] However this point of interpretation needs further scrutiny, but from the stand point of my thesis, the essential task is to establish the link between the *theory of recollection, the method of midwifery,* and *the technique of refutation.* This will go a long towards establishing the relevance of the *Meno* from the point of view of later

Platonic doctrines regarding the soul and its innate knowledge of Form.

We may however conclude from the above discussion, how Socrates successfully established the unity amongst his dialogues through the above-mentioned methods. Form this, one more point may be concluded that Socrates purposefully avoided the discussion of recollection in other dialogues and logically established the link through other similar methods, such as midwifery and Elenchus. All these have been done only to strengthen his belief that knowledge is innate. By means of Midwifery and Cross examining by the refutation he leads towards something, which is innate. The important hypothesis of the *Meno* is "Is virtue teacheable ?". There also applying this technique, he advocated that in order to make men virtous one must make them know what virtue is, one must remove their false opinions they have about it. And in order to remove such false opinions, one must subject them to Elenchus; in order to lead them to that part of knowledge which is innate.

If we consider the recollection theory both in the *Meno* and *Phaedo* we find both are certainly different. In the *Phaedo*, the theory of recollection is discussed by Cebes and Simmias is completely different from Meno with Socrates. In the *Meno* while Socrates by putting the right question at the right time, helped the slave-boy in recollecting the geometrical truths, which according to him innately there in the human mind, never, however adopted the technique of *recollection by association*, rather that was completely a type of *direct recollection*. But in the *Phaedo* the discussion of recollection appeared in the form of association. The recollection by association is, if *x* is associated with *y*, then the perception of *x*, reminds one of *y*, as because one is associated with the other and similarly in the case of difference. The theory of recollection taken both in the *Meno* and *Phaedo*, thus demonstrates further that in the *Meno* the recollection depends only on how the question is being put, it plays the role of an efficient cause, whereas in the *Phaedo* we find sense-experience also has got its role in recollection. From this it may be concluded that according to the *Phaedo* even in the case of empirical knowledge, one cannot forget the role of recollection.

(v) Conclusion

Before concluding this chapter, I would like to discuss the question, what is recollected ? Is it of Platonic Forms ? This question becomes important because Plato does not discuss these in any dialogue, he gives an account of recollection in the *Meno* and regarding Forms in the *Phaedo*. We may presuppose that as the *Meno* was an earlier dialogue of Plato, which was in some sense pre-mature, performed only the role of answering the Sophists, hence in this dialogue, there is no discussion regarding Forms. In order to substantiate this point further the discussion of R.E. Allen's views[18] are essential. He has made it clear that in early,as well as the middle dialogues of Plato we find the existence of Forms.[19] He has also mentioned that—"the theory of Forms in the middle dialogues is meant to answer questions, especially questions arising out of problems of knowledge, which the early dialogues have not yet raised."[20] He has also referred to the theory of recollection in particular. He continued further :

> "The middle dialogues do not abondon that 'what is it ?' question. They pursue it in the light of a new ontology. That ontology rests on two principles, the immortality and the divinity of the rational soul; and the complete reality and eternity of the objects of knowledge. These principles in F.M. Conford's phrase, are the pillars of platonism and their architrave is the doctrine of recollection, the doctrine that the truth of things is always in the soul. The foundation on which this lofty structure rests is a theory of Forms which implies the diminished reality and deficiency of resemblance of sensible objects."[21]

Form the above it becomes clear that the recollection doctrine aims at only recollection of Forms and nothing else. As we find the presence of recollection in the dialogues of Plato, starting from earlier to the later ones[22] and as it is established that it is only Forms that can be recollected, therefore in the *Meno*, it may be concluded that it was the Forms which are being recollected by the slave-boy and those Forms are there innately in the human mind.

Form the above discussion we may arrive at a central question that, if it is only Forms that are the objects of recollection, then if we give up Forms, should we give up the theory of recollection also ? My thesis in this context aims at a positive answer. In order to justify this issue, a discussion of Aristotle would be of much value. In the early period of Aristotle, he was generally in agreement with Plato. As Plato argued for the immortality of soul in the *Phaedo*, similarly Aristole in the *Eudemus* reached an identical solution.[23] Jaeger showed that in the *Eudemus*, Aristotle expressed a purely Platonic theory of the soul, he even gave an account showing that *Protrepticus* also was throughly Platonic in nature. Further he showed that in the *De-Philosophia* Aristole in many respects became critical of Platonism. Therefore the young Aristole first followed the line of recollection, but the moment he clearly grasped the logical nature of pure-thought and realised that memory is a psychological phenomenon, he denied that *Nus* was capable of recollection and dropped pre-existence and immortality.[24] First he did accept transcendent Forms of Plato both in *Protrepticus* as well as in the *Eudemus*,[25] but later on when he became critical of Plato, he had given up both. This very well justifies the relation between the theory of recollection with that of theory of Forms. Therefore Jaeger had rightly remarked that—"Even if Proclus' quotation did not explicitly guarantee the occurrence of the Forms in the *Eudemus* the adoption of the doctrines of pre-existence and recollection would be enough by itself to make them necessary. As Plato says in the *Phaedo*, you can admit or deny the Forms, but you cannot separate them from recollection and pre-existence. These doctrines stand or fall together, and the necessity for both of them is one and the same. Later on, when Aristole abandoned the theory of Forms, he inevitably dropped recollection along with it.[26]

The Platonic search for attainment of knowledge, which is carried on thoughout almost all of the dialogues, seems to hold as evident that the knowledge is innate, because if at all we assume that there is knowledge and again if we assume that knowledge is not possible by sense-experience, for which the entire *Theatetus* is devoted, then the obvious conclusion would be that knowledge is obtained through non-empirical means, and the primary aim of the subsequent chapters of the thesis would be to explore the possibilities of that non-empirical means of knowledge and its philosophical significance.

REFERENCES

1. Though I have used the *a priori* in the context of Plato, that term was not found in the writings of Plato. I have used that taking the meaning which was of late discovered and I would explain that in due course.
2. Ross, W. D., *Plato's Theory of Ideas*, (Clarendon Press, Oxford, 1951), p. 35.
3. For further discussion see "The Reciprocity Argument and the Structure of Plato's *Phaedo*", by Kenneth Dorter, *Journal of the History of Philosophy*, vol. XV, No. 1, January (1977) pp. 1-11.
4. R. S. Bluck, *Plato's Phaedo*, Routledge and Kegan Paul, London, 1955, p. 19.
5. Cf. Op. cit., R. S. Bluck, *Plato's Phaedo*, The Argument from Affinity (78B-84B), pp. 73-84.
6. For detailed information see G. Vlastos, *Platonic Studies*, Princeton University Press, 1973, pp. 76-110.
7. N. Gulley, *Plato's Theory of Knowledge*, Methuen, London, 1962, p. 87.
8. For further reference see, "Anemnesis: Platonic Doctrine or Sophistic Absurdity?" Cobb, William S. Jr., *Dialogue* (1973) Vol. XII, No. 4, pp. 604-628.
9. Crombie, I. M., Plato, *The midwife's Apprentice* (Routledge and Kegan Paul, London: 1964) p. 5.
   (a) *Plainly Early Dialogues*—Apology, Charmides, Crito, Euthyphro, Gorgias, *Ion, Laches, *Lovers (or Rivals), Lysis, Menexenus, + Meno, Protagoras.
   (b) *Neither plainly early nor plainly Late*
   +Cratylus, +Euthydenus, Permenides, Phaedo, Phaedrus, Republic, Symposium (or Banquet), Theaetetus, +Timaeus, Critias.
   Plainly Late—*Epinomis, Laws, Philebus, Sophist, Statesman (or Politicus).
   * =authenticity disputed; + =grouping disputed.
10. *Ibid.*, p. 5 (See the classification).
11. F. M. Cornford, *Plato's Theory of Knowledge.* (Routledge and Kegan Paul, London: 1960) p. 17.
12. Ibid., pp. 27-28.
13. Ibid., p. 5
14. Elenchus also occurs in the late Sophist (229E-230E). But Elenchus has undergone some change in the middle and later dialogues. "Thus Elenchus changes into dialectic, the negative into the posi-

tive, pedagogy into discovery, morality into science", Robinson remarked. For reference please see, *The Philosophy of Socrates, A collection of Critical Essays*, edited by G. Vlastos, 1971, Anchor Books, pp. 78-93.

15. Ibid., p. 78.
16. Ibid., p. 91.
17. Ibid., p. 91.
18. Ibid., pp. 319-334.
19. Ibid., "It assumes the existence of Forms, as Universals, standards, and essences. That assumption is stated or implied throughout the early dialogues." pp. 328-329.
20. Ibid., p. 333.
21. Ibid., p. 334.
22. Paul Shorey, *Unity of Plato's Thought*, (Chicago Press: 1960) p. 44. The doctrine of (Anemnesis), then represented in the *Politicus*, is not abondened in the *Philebus.* This conclusion might have been affirmed *a priori*. For 'recollection', once indissolubly associated with the ideas and the pre-existence of the soul, would not be given up while they were retained. But pre-existence is assumed in the *Laws*, and the ideas, as we have seen, occur in the *Politicus* and are reaffirmed in the *Timaeus*, which also implies the soul's prior knowledge of all things, in language recalling the *Phaedrus* and *Politicus*.
23. Werner, Jaeger, *Aristotle. Fundamentals of the History of His Development*, (Oxford University Press, 1962) ff. 39, and During, and,
    G. E. L. Owen, edited, *Aristotle and Plato in Mid-fourth Century*, Goteborg, 1960; may be conferred for further information, ff. 191.
24. Op. Cit., W. Jaeger, p. 52.
25. Op. Cit., During and Owen, pp. 253-254.
26. Op. Cit., Jaeger, p. 52.

2

The Problem of Innateness in Medieval Philosophy:

Some Aspects from St. Augustine to St. Thomas Aquinas

(i) St. Augustine's Doctrine of Divine Illumination

At one time there was a wide spread impression that the student of philosophy could very well jump straight from Plato and Aristotle to Bacon and Descartes, omitting consideration of Post-Aristotelian Greek Thought and of Medieval Philosophy. The philosophy of Middle Ages was considered to be dependent on christian theology; it was also a common prevalent idea that no logical development of any value had been undertaken during this period. If anybody was interested in metaphysical speculation, one tended to eliminate Medieval speculation as theology and turn to Descartes, Spinoza and Leibniz. If one wanted a philosophical tradition based on experience, one turned to British Empiricism. If it was Logic, then from Aristotle to the logical developments of Modern times. In all these aspects, Medieval period was thought to be completely dark without making any contribution to Philosophy and Logic. But present day scholarship has removed the so-called darkness and given us a better understanding of the continuity of Ancient, Medieval, Renaissance and Modern Philosophy. Therefore while giving an account of the concept of innateness, I would like to give due consideration to the thinkers of the Medieval period along with others. Particularly here I wish to explain the views of three main representatives of Medieval thought, St. Augustine, St. Bonaventure, and St. Thomas Aquinas.

St. Augustine, in order to find out a solution to scepticism, found the Platonic tradition to be of a great value. He started his theory of knowledge, which is quite rational and non-sensuous having a Platonic cast. Plato's teaching that there are two worlds, an intelligible world of Forms and the world of sensibles influenced Augustine to such an extent that even without any revision he endorsed Plato's assertion of the existence of an intelligible world, by which, he meant the eternal and unchanging reason whereby God made the world. He had identified the Platonic intelligible world of Forms with the Divine mind containing the archetypal ideas of all its creatures, that is the creative wisdom and word (Logos) of God. Augustine describes our knowledge of this intelligible world as analogous to sight, so that he advocates—'Under standing is the same thing for the mind as seeing is for the bodily senses', or 'reason is the mind's sight, whereby it perceives truth through itself, without the body's intervention.'[1]

In order to oppose Academic scepticism regarding the impossibility of knowledge, he accepted propositions of mathematics and logic as indubitable truths. He opinion is that these types of proposition are primarily there in the mind. They have the characteristics of universality, necessity and immutability for which sense experience can do nothing, because according to him sense cognition is not perfectly safe, for the following reasons:

Firstly—its proper function is to warn the soul of some changes that take place in the body rather to represent to it the nature of things, and

Secondly—this nature of material things, is itself a changeable one; from these two reasons we can conclude that no pure truth can be expected from sensations.[2] Because sense knowledge does not rise above the level of opinion; it has not the value of truth, for it is transient like its object, and depend upon corporeal organ, where as truth itself is immutable. So he concluded that such truths were known independently of sense-experience, that is through an analogous type of experience known as intellectual 'sight'. Augustine even included the statements of moral and aesthetic value judgement and indeed the whole realm of 'wisdom' as eternal truths and identified them with the archetypal ideas of the Divine mind. He also argued that since the soul is the cause of its sensation, it is also the cause of its intellectual cognition. On this point, Augustine emphasised the fact that there is more in intellectual knowledge than in either the thing or the mind. Therefore rational knowledge is the only true knowledge, which is the aim of Augustine's epistemology. Hence like Plato, Augustine, advocates that the contents of the intelligible are known by the mind independently of sense-experience. Augustine referred to the slave-boy of the *Meno* and argued that the light of the eternal reason is present with the boy, it is not that once he knew them and has forgotten them as Plato accepted, rather the knowledge of the eternal truths is not the result of the re-discovery of a residual deposit left in the mind from a previous existence, but is the work of continuous discovery by the mind. This happens by means of the intellectual light, which is always present to it and is its means of contact with the world of intelligible reality. But what exactly the content of the know-ledge made accessible by this intellectual illumination was, a question difficult to decide. Whether that illumination provides the concepts with which the mind works in its interpretation of sense-experience or it provides the mind with a yard-stick by which to regulate its judgements.[3] From our point of view, it is not necessary here to answer what is that content of know-ledge; it is enough to support my thesis that the content of knowledge is innate. Gilson, the prominent scholar in Augusti-nism, advocates that 'innatism' has no place in the doctrine of St. Augustine, because in Augustinism, it is through the senses that the soul knows things relating to body, and through itself that it knows things relating to the mind.

Though Augustine tried to eliminate the doctrine of innatism still we find two important connotations of this term remain applicable to him. In the first place, it is legitimate, to attribute a certain innatism in the sense that the term indicates an opposition to Aristotelian empiricism, which advocates that knowledge is possible only through sense-experience.

Secondly, we can say that in Augustinism, any knowledge, whether its object is corporeal or incorporeal, implies an innate element to the extent that it is a truth. So far as these two opinions are concerned, Gilson also points out that they are not innate because, "the truth is not born in us nor with us, although it preceds our birth and has attended us from birth, nor does it come from within, although it is there that we find it and through there it must pass."[4] From the discussion of Gilson the problem arises of finding out the unique relationship which we call neither extrinsic nor intrinsic. Here 'intrinsic' has been taken as a substitute for 'innatism'. Perhaps this question can be answered after we have examined the celebrated Augustinian doctrine of Divine illumination.

St. Augustine had taken the metaphor of illumination as a distinctive feature, so that his theory of knowledge is commonly known as "The Augustinian doctrine of Divine illumination of the intellect." In protest against sceptics, Augustine considered intelligible truth as the best safe-guard. Therefore his doctrine of the Divine illumination remained for him the decisive moment in his own liberation from scepticism.

This illumination assumes that, as the sun is the source of physical light which makes things visible, so God is the source of spiritual light which makes the sciences intelligible to the mind. Thus God is to our mind what the sun is to our sight; as the sun is the source of light so God is the source of truth. Since the truth is necessary, immutable and eternal, it cannot be obtained from the things and the mind, because they are contingent, since they all begin and end in time. Hence it is only possible from God, who is immutable and eternal. In other words, the demonstration of God's existence can be considered as included in the epistemology of St. Augustine. There must be a cause which makes us all see the truth at the same time in the same way. God is the inner master who teaches the same truth to all the minds that seek after it. He is the intelligible sun, which enlightens the minds of all men. Thus, in Augustinism God becomes the Father of intelligible light and Father of our illumination. God has made the mind a receiver of intellectual illumination. He has also made the will the receiver of moral illumination through the intellectual illumination of mind. To make it more precise, his theory of knowledge holds that objects are neither innate in the soul, nor are they formed from sense-perception by the activity of any abstractive faculty. They are 'irradiated into' the soul, 'participated' by created beings, and 'illuminated' for the mind's perception by a Divine light. What is that light? It is neither mystical nor supernatural since all men possess it, at least in a rudimentary form. Nor is it like any physical light on the one hand, and uncreated light on the other. It is something of which the presence is demanded by the analysis of reason.

The intellectual mind which Augustine assigns to man, can be called a natural light, which would never violate his thought. The result of Divine illumination is not a supernatural illumination rather by definition it belongs to the nature of the human intellect. Thus God does not take the place of our intellect when we think the truth. His illumination is needed only to make our intellect capable of thinking the truth. Augustine demonstrates that this Divine light is present in everyman who comes into this world, it is never absent from us, even if we neglect it. Therefore man is endowed with an intellect, he is by nature being illumined by God, therefore there is no question of claiming that this is mystical.

How is this doctrine of illumination brought to the human mind? The chief characteristics of illumination is its immediacy; it acts directly on the soul, it is in this way that God presides over the human mind. Augustine advocates that although the soul is not God, it is very near to God. As the soul is subject to God, so it is subject to certain 'intelligible realities' which are the Divine ideas themselves. Those Divine ideas again subsist in God, therefore the human intellect is immediately subject to God's ideas, which are eternal, unchangeable and necessary. We see these truths in the Divine truth itself and due to this Divine truth, we conceive truth in ourselves, which establishes a direct contact between God and the human mind. It is an ontological dependence, of the human intellect with respect to God, from which it derives its being, activity and truth. If God's action ceases. His creatures cease to act and if the illuminating presence of truth is withdrawn from man, he is plunged at once into darkness.

From the above exposition, we may conclude that to see the ideas of God would be to see God. God knows all, including material things *a priori* because they are merely copies of His ideas. Thus if we had full knowledge of God's ideas, we should know material things without having any perception of them. The work of sensations are only to call us back to the inner light and that inner sense not only perceives what is presented by the body's senses, but also perceives these senses themselves which proves its dominant nature. Therefore the Augustinian doctrine of illumination cannot be interpreted as an intuition of the content of God's ideas. Hence a necessary cooperation between Divine illumination, human intellect and bodily senses are required for knowledge of external things. But what is the share that we should assign to each of these causes in the formation of our ideas? Whether like Plato, Augustine does see this sensation only as an occasion of remembering the idea or does he see in it a kind of matter from which our intellect extracts the idea, like Aristotle? According to the opinion of Gilson, it is neither.[5] Rather he advocates that we discover truth not in memories deposited previously in the soul like Plato, but in the Divine light which is constantly present there.

In comparison to Aristotle, the sensation in Augustinism is something very different from sensation in Aristotelism. According to Augustine, sensation is an action exercised by the soul, but in Aristotle it is a passion undergone by the soul. So in Augustine's opinion the Divine illumination deals with intelligibles to the exclusion of sensibles.

To give a final shape to the origin of ideas according to Augustine, it, is found, that he admitted, that man has a whole range of ideas which are completely independent of any sensible source, such as number, the good, the true, the beautiful, equality, likeness, wisdom etc. Now since Augustine not only denies any empirical origin but also rejects the doctrine of innatism, in the strict sense of the term, and the pre-existence of soul, which it entails, can we think of any other origin for the content of our concepts except the Divine illumination? The answer would be, according to Augustine that knowledge is impressed on us by Divine illumination and all we know is that illumination gives us 'notions' of non-empirical origin.[6] And these notions, the human mind achieves when the mind participates in the eternal truth, which is there in the form of natural light. This way of analysing the origin of ideas seems that as if Augustine wants to reduce the doctrine of innatism to the Divine illumination.

However, from the theory of Divine illumination, it is understood, that things are to be known by means of illumination, therefore, Augustine eliminated the idea of innatism from his epistemology, but when we consider that from the stand point of the human mind, it seems evident that ideas are there innately in the human mind. The only thing that man has to do is to remember or rather to recollect the knowledge which is present there by virtue of its nature. Therefore, Armstrong has rightly remarked that, "Augustine's *memoria* is, in the first place, equivalent of Plato's anamnesis."[7] This reference to the Platonic theory of anemnesis shows how the epistemology of Augustine indirectly pre-supposes the doctrine of innatism. Even, F. Copleston writes, "For the Platonic theory of reminiscence he substituted his own theory of Divine illumination, an illumination which enables us not only to see, eternal truths but also to judge of things in relation to eternal standards or ideas".[8] And it is Platonism again, Copleston remarked elsewhere, which inspires hs theory of knowledge.[9]

Augustine's explanation as to the actualisation of knowledge from its contents involves minds' symbol-making activity and also pre-supposes the doctrine of innatism. With regard to this concept of symbol-making activity, Augustine compares the mind with the eye in this respect. The mind can see the ideas with its inner and intelligible eye. This outlook of Augustine's epistemology indicates how the ideas are there innately and because of the illumination of the mind we usually recollect them.

If we follow the philosophy of St. Augustine further, some partinent questions may arise. Augustine rejected at the outset the empiricism of Aristotle and scepticism by taking a stand like Descartes, who vehemently criticised the sceptics; therefore, Augustine adovocates that, "I known that I am because I know that I think and I live." Even the most extreme scepticism cannot possibly deny this, and since I know myself directly as a knowing being, this is exactly what I am."[10]

Attention has often been called to the close similarity

between "*Si enim fall-or, sum*" (If I am deceived, I am), of Augustine and the *Cogito, ergo sum* of Descartes,[11] which means that consciousness gives us certitude of the reality of the thinking ego. This attitude of St. Augustine directly proves that he was being influenced by Platonic rationalism instead of empiricistic trend; therefore, like Plato and Descartes, Augustine himself considered intelligible truth as the best safeguard against scepticism. The above adherence of Augustine proves that the concept of innatism prevails in his entire explanation of human knowledge in its own way.

A surprising question emerges out of St. Augustine, why he preferred the language, of illumination language instead of innatism? It is a fact that he never advocates anywhere, knowledge in terms of innate ideas, rather he very much emphasises illumination, which has been already mentioned elsewhere. If we subtantiate this point further, we find that St. Augustine was bound to adhere to that, because of his conception of philosophy. His acceptance of God as the eternal and immutable being demonstrates further that He is all the intelligible patterns, or 'reasons', of all that which is capable of existence and these eternal intelligible patterns or models are called Divine ideas,[12] and this notion of Divine word, which conceived ideas after whose pattern God has created the world, has become the common property of all Christian theology. That Divine word is the light of the world, because He is the source of its intelligibility of its beauty. Precisely then that, Divine word is the light of human minds. Plato, and after him Plotinus, had clearly advocated that, in a world where things are but images, true knowledge is impossible unless the knowing intellect relates things to their models, which are the Divine ideas. Therefore, Augustine advocates that, men can only know in sharing themselves with the Divine word and that is possible only through the Divine illumination, which comes from above. Hence, he writes, the truth of our knowledge rests upon God. This analysis reveals, why Augustine preferred illumination instead of innatism.

If once again we go back to the origin and nature of the theory of illumination, we find one more additional point to the above exposition. The theory of illumination, for the first time played a major part in the philosophy of Plato. In the *Seventh letter* (341 C, 344 B),] there is mention of a sudden flash of understanding or insight in the mind as a flood of light. In the *Republic,* Plato employed the analogy of light and vision to describe the process of understanding or of knowledge in general (Books V—VIII). Understanding, here depends on the intellectual illumination of the mind and its objects, just as vision depends on a physical illumination of the eye and its objects. The illumination theory whtch has been exposed by Plato in the *Seventh letter,* was never based on any mystical ground, therefore, Augustine's account of the theory is free from any mystical interpretation. In Christian thought, particularly in St. Augustine, this theory of illumination is again found in its most highly developed form. Like Plato, Augustine thought of understanding as analogous to seeing. Understanding or intellectual insight, was, therefore, he held, conditional or illumination, just as physical sight was, only here the light was the intelligible light, that emanated from the Divine mind and in illuminating the human mind it endowed it with understanding. And this understanding was an inward participation of the human mind in the Divine. This brief recapitulation of the theory of illumination suggests, how it aims at an activity. In many passages, the illuminative action of God signifies the creative act, to which the soul and the intellect owe their reality.[13] Therefore, it has been rightly remarked that, "His illuminating activity gathers and re-unites all that it touches, it prefects creatures endowed with reason and understanding by uniting them with the one pervading light."[14] This nature of illumination theory, which aims at a type of Divine act, opposes radically the theory of innatism. Because the innatism theory suggests that the concepts are primodially inherent in the human mind, which is independent of sense-experience, it only needs revelation of them by means of proper questioning, which is only a passive phenomenan, not an active one, for this reason Augustine preferred the language of illumination instead of innatism. The differences between innatism and illumination theory seem to be only of methodological, but the content of that methodology is same, that the knowledge is innate. In other words, so far as it remains in the human level we speak of it as innate, but if we extend it further to the level of God, as is done by Augustine, it must be in the language of illumination.

St. Augustine's preference of illumination to innatism, reminds us, for the exact position of Kant to his predecessors. That is to say, the rejection of innate ideas by Locks and Artistotle etc., resulted in empiricism, but in the case of Kant, it is not *empiricism* rather it is in the sense of active consciousness of the mind. Kant does not accept the doctrine of innatism, rather he advocates that something is innate in terms of dynamic consciousness. If we see both Plato and Augustine, we find the same method being applied. Plato's acceptance of innate ideas, as a passive disposition, and Augustine's acceptance of that in terms of illumination, pre-supposes a situation like that of Kant. Rather the tendency to avoid the term innatism becomes prominent only in Kant. Therefore, apart from theology, both Augustine and Kant seem to be in the same line of thought, when both do not use innatism in preference to other concepts: In case of Kant, knowledge is the product of mental activity while Augustine, holds that it is the product of Divine illumination because of his religious tendency.

(ii) St. Bonaventure

The key to the understanding of St. Bonaventure's theory of knowledge, as Prof. Gilson has shown, lies in his interpretation of St. Augustine's doctrine of Divine-illumination.[15] Because St. Bonaventure intellectually and spiritually was a disciple of St. Augustine. St. Bonaventure, profitted much from Augustinian way of thought. This would become clear when we go through the philosophy of St. Bonaventure. He builds his philosophical system on three most significant doctrines of St. Augustine.

1. The metaphysic of light.
2. The Divine illumination of the intellect.
3. The seminal tendencies in matter.

The first and the second are in origin Platonic, third, is a Platonic suggestion but amplified by the Stoics. However, my concern would be to concentrate on Divine illumination of the intellect, because it is this doctrine, which influenced the theory of knowledge of St. Bonaventure.

St. Bonaventure advocates that the human knowledge is possible because of the Divine Light which is present within us. We see the truth both in and by the eternal ideas. St. Bonaventure was very careful here, to point out that this does not involve the view, that the eternal ideas are seen by us as they exist in God, they appear to us as faint reflections due to the sin of man. In the state of innocence, the human race enjoyed complete knowledge in the contemplation of God but sin produced a defect in human understanding, so that it is always partial and incomplete.

Corporeal things, as perceived by sense and impressions gained from sense-experience stored in memory form the data from which universal ideas are abstracted. Here St. Bonaventure is just as emphatic as Aquinas in declaring that without sense-perception, our knowledge of natural objects would be impossible. But, St. Bonaventure will not agree that all knowledge springs from sense-experience. The knowledge that the soul gains of itself and of God, is not due to the agency of sense; here an interior illumination is necessary. To deny this is to ignore the operation of the interior light. St. Bonaventure seems therefore, to reconcile the Aristotelian doctrine of sensation conceived as a passion undergone by the human compound with the Augustinian and Plotinian theory of sensation conceived as an action of the soul.

So far as St. Bonaventure's analysis of knowledge situation is concerned, sensible images are the data from which the intellect gets its intelligible knowledge and the abstraction is the work of possible intellect which carries out the necessary operation for retaining only the common and universal elements of these particular data. Each human soul has, in addition to its own possible intellect. its own agent intellect whose function is to illuminate the possible intellect and helps in doing effective abstraction. Agent intellect and possible intellect are fundamentally two distinct functions of one and the same soul, in its effort to assimilate intelligible in the sensible. This effort of abstraction is not always necessary, it is required only for acquisition of scientific knowledge, not for wisdom. The sensible knowledge helps in knowing the natural aspect of nature. When we go beyond sensible objects, we call upon an inner-light which perceived in the principles of the sciences and the natural truth innate in man. The Divine light helps us to know them, in which the sensibility has no part to play. Here St. Bonaventure does not confuse philosophies, rather he is in full awareness of what he is doing, attempting a synthesis of Plato and Aristotle. Therefore, he asserts that neither Plato nor Aristotle expressed the whole truth about the knowledge. He stated, Aristotle used the language of science, while Plato that of wisdom. but St. Augustine inspired by the Holy Spirit speaks the language of both. If one considers things by sense and the lower power of the sense, he achieves only a relative certitude, but when one turns from Nature to God, he receives from Him an absolute certitude.[16] Thus, St. Bonaventure wanted to promote a tradition of a synthesis which St. Augustine had already achieved.

St. Augustine had been able to realise this above synthesis because of the doctrine of illumination, and St. Bonaventure also transmitted the same to his school. It consists in explaining the presence of the truth in human thought by the immediate action of Divine ideas on our intellect. How then, does the human intellect attain an absolutely certain knowledge? Such knowledge presents two characteristics:

1. It is immutable as concerns the object known; and
2. Infallible as concerns subject knowing.

Now the man is neither an infallible knowing subject nor are the objects he attains immutable in nature. If at all the human intellect possesses intellectual certitude, it is because of the Divine ideas themselves which are immutable intelligibles, illumine the human intellect in its knowledge of such objects. Because the mind is able to realise the truth of a thing understood by virtue of an innate light which is a reflection of the Divine ideas, this light supplies a standard and criterion of truth and that truth we can only see by the illumination of the Divine ideas.

This above exposition clearly justifies, how St. Bonaventure, was exactly in the line of the Augustinian tradition, as to support the illumination theory, which ultimately resulted in the acceptance of a doctrine akin to the doctrine of innatism. Therefore, it has been rightly remarked that—"The powerful influence of St. Augustine of St. Bonaventure's thought should certainly not be underestimated".[17]

St. Bonaventure accepts the Aristotelian distinction between possible or passive and Active intellect. He tells us that this possible intellect is not purely passive; it has the power of turning towards the intelligible, which is contained in the sensible species. It abstracts and judges by the assistance it receives from active intellect. Similarly the active intellect is not completely in act. It cannot understand anything in virtue of its own powers and requires the help of the species which is held in the imagination. In accepting the complete structure of knowledge of Aristotle, both passive and Active intellect etc., St. Bonaventure never did any prejudice to St. Augustine, rather he interpreted, the Aristotelian structure of knowledge in terms of Augustinian Divine illumination. F.C. Copleston, therefore, says—"A theory of perception which is largely Aristotelian is combined with the Augustinian doctrine of Divine Illumination."[18]

To St. Bonaventure, knowledge of the soul and God present a different problem. The question is, 'can one know a virtue of the soul such as charity: If the subject already has it, he needs nothing besides it to enable him to know it.' But let us suppose that he does not possess charity. He cannot know it through a direct intuition of its essence, because charity is not present in the soul. Nor can he know it by means of an image derived from sense-experience, for virtues are not objects of sense-perception. Therefore, the only solution is to assume that our knowledge comes about through a species which is innate.[19] Even in the same way, the knowledge of God cannot be gained by means of sensible images nor through a direct intuition, rather it is implicit in the rational soul. Hence St. Bonaventure asserts that, "the existence of God is a truth implanted in the human mind. He does not mean by this that human beings have an innate idea of God or an inborn explicit knowledge of Him. He means that man has implicit awareness of God which can be made explicit by reflection.[20] This remark of Copleston, inspite of its polemic seems to suggest that the idea of God is actually innate. His very statement that, the man has an implicit awareness of God which can be made explicit by reflection provides enough ground to accept the above view. In support to this thesis, it has been said, "The human soul knows God simply by reflecting on itself, since it is made in the image of God the knowledge by which it knows, the desire by which it loves, the memory by which it grasps and possesses itself, tend towards God, suppose and imply Him necessarily; the innateness of its knowledge of Him consists then in the power which it possesses of forming this knowledge without requiring fresh resources from the external world."[21]

However, we can now at least assume that St. Bonaventure in his theory of knowledge pre-supposes an element of innatism because of his adherence to doctrine of Divine illumination. His acceptance of soul in relation to God and God itself revealed very much his own stand. His journey of soul towards God by means of Divine illumination and the cooperation of God in construction of knowledge justified his own acceptance to the doctrine of innatism. If we take a look at the philosophy of St. Bonaventure with that of Aquinas, we find that Bonaventure differed from him in the attitude towards human intellectual activity. Since the soul and its power make up a self sufficient unity, there can be no direct impact of external material objects upon the soul or its powers; sense-perception is a purely bodily function. The knowledge of God is innate, whereas the knowledge of external being comes to the soul from without and indirectly, by means of a judgment upon the experience of the corporeal senses. The Thomistic intellect forms intelligibles out of sense-impressions and creates the first principles, which builds an entire edifice of knowledge, while St. Bonaventure's intellect finds within itself the intelligible which it has not formed out of sense perception but has received from one within it who is more "within" than its own interior life.[22] The difference which St. Bonaventure maintained with Aquinas clearly revealed, how the doctrine of Divine illumination has gone deep to his philosophy as a consequence of which strong critics like Aristotle and Aquinas could never shake his being a disciple of St. Augustine.

If we follow the doctrine of innatism from Plato to St. Bonaventure, we ffnd a conceptual change in it. In case of Plato, we assume, the doctrine of innate ideas in the form of recollection, which we have to recollect by means of suitable questioning. While St. Augustine, being an orthodox christian theologian, he assumed it in the form of Divine illumination. It is because of this Divine light we used to see things, the individual soul independently cannot construct any knowledge; it is because of the flash of light which comes from Divine, the soul used to be lighted. Therefore, we find in Augustine, the innatism doctrine which was completely passive suddenly appears in the form of an active agency. It is that active agency, by which the individual soul gets its knowledge which is innately there. Wnen we come to St. Bonaventure again we find a conceptual change, however, having the same content. Bonaventure's introduction of Aristotle in his theory of knowledge demonstrates further that Divine illumination is not totally a concept of mystical origin with a theological content, rather it has an origin in the empirical realm. Therefore, St. Bonaventure interpreted Aristotle's passive and Active intellect in an Augustinian way.

However, St. Bonaventure, while struggling in between St. Augustine and Aristotle, endeavoured to give a new direction to the doctrine of innate-ideas. It is found that St. Bonaventure's aquisition of knowledge of sensible objects more or less closely in the line of Aristotle. Aristotle admits that the soul in regard to knowledge of such objects is originally a *tabula-rasa*, and he has no place for innate ideas. This rejection of innate ideas applies also to our knowledge of first principles. Some are of the opinion that these principles are innate in the Active intellect, though acquired as far as the possible intellect is concerned; but such a theory agrees neither with the words of Aristotle nor with the truth. For, if these principles are innate in the Active-intellect, why then are they not communicated to the passive intellect without the help of the senses, and why does it not know these principles from the very beginning? A modified version of innatism holds, that the principles are innate in their most general form while the conclusions or particular applications are acquired, but here it would be difficult to show why a child does not know the first principles in their general form. Moreover, even this modified innatism contradicts both Aristotle and Augustine. Within this crisis Bonaventure considered that a theory which united against it both Aristotle and Augustine could not possibly be true. It remains then to say that the principles are innate only in the sense that the intellect is endowed with a natural light, which enables it to apprehend the principles in their universality when it has acquired knowledge of the relevant species or ideas. For example, no one knows what a whole is or a part, until he has acquired it by means of sense perception, but once he has acquired the idea, the light of the intellect enables him to apprehend the principle that the whole is greater than the part. In this point Bonaventure is at one with Thomas Acquinas. Bonaventure, employed this notion of innatism in case of knowledge of God and knowledge of vitrue. He argued that the knowledge of God and virtue are innate, not in the sense that everyman has knowledge of them from the very beginning, but there is present in the soul a natural light by which it can recognise truth. He claimed further that the soul has all the material to form the idea without its recourse to the sensible world. Hence, we find that Bonaventure maintained a theory what we may call a theory of virtually innateness. This theory bears some resemblance to the theories put forward at a later time by Descartes and Leibniz.[23]

(iii) St. Thomas Aquinas

St. Thomas Aquinas, one of the prominent philosophers of the medieval period would be of great value in a discussion of the concept of innateness and its role in the Post-Platonic period. While discussing Thomas Aquinas' theory of knowledge, we have to discuss his psychology and ethics, because in him they all originated in the same ground. If we start the analysis of knowledge since Plato, we have an interesting development in Thomas Aquinas. Plato, particularly in the *Meno*, which I have already discussed, advocates that, the soul understands corporeal knowledge through innate species. But Aquinas, being influenced by Aristotle adopted the view that the intellect by which the soul understands has no innate species. Going against the Platonic tradition, Aqninas argued that if the soul has the natural knowledge of all things, it would be impossible for the soul to forget the existence of such knowledge. For no man forgets what he knows actually. Secondly, he argued that, if a sense be wanting, the knowledge of what is apprehended through that sense is also wanting. For example, a man who is born blind can have no knowledge of colours. This would not be the case if the soul had innate likenesses of all intelligible things. Therefore, Aquinas concluded that the soul does not know corporeal things through innate species. So far it is clearly seen that Aquinas was in the Aristotelian tradition and completely influenced by Aristotle, but if we proceed further into the psychological as well as ethical aspects of Aquinas, which are intimately connected with that of human understanding, we find a suggestion to the effect that the influence of Aristotle over Aquinas may not be a strong one. Because it has also been remarked that Aquinas conceives of no middle term between sensualism and Platonism, namely that "Innateism" of the intellect without an "innateism" of principles, which describes exactly St. Thomas' position. Therefore, the often accepted influence of Aristotle over Aquinas becomes a debatable point. Rather, it seems, he was through out in an Augustinian tradition. As a matter of fact, we see there are a good many elements in his thonght which originally came from other sources than Aristotle. A simple example is the talk about the Divine ideas, which obviously derives from St. Augustine.[24] If we compare St. Augustine with Aquinas, one is no better than the other. Between their wisdom, there is not only agreement and harmony but a fundamental unity.[25] Therefore, it has been rightly remarked by Maritain that, "He (Thomas Aquinas) corrects Aristotle, he honours Augustine as a son honours his father."[26] Even his own commentry on Aristotle remarked that it was erratic.[27] Rather both Augustine and Aquinas were very much close in their thought process. Therefore. Father Gardeil remarked—"The positions on which they differ can be counted; it is impossible to number those in which they agree."[28] Again it would be foolishness to oppose Thomism and Augustinism, as though they were two opposed systems. The first is a system, second is not. Thomism is the scientific state of christian wisdom; among the fathers and in St. Augustine that wisdom is still in its source.[29] It is sometimes remarked that Thomas Aquinas preferred to be in the Platonic tradition than in that of Aristotle in the point of dispute.[30] Regarding Thomas' affinity to Plato, if we substantiate further, we find clear indications. Even Thomas himself did not forget to compare Aristotle, the so called mentor of his philosophy with Plato. He advocates that there is a fundamental agreement between Plato and Aristotle. This agreement is born out of the notion of *participation.* Thomas also accepted the metaphysical nucleus of the Platonic notion of *Participation, composition of esse and .essence and doctrine of analogy.*

Thomas accepted that corporeal objects act upon the organs of sense and sensation is a composite act of body and soul, not of the soul alone using a body, as accepted by Augustine. The senses of the human understanding apprehended only the particulars, but they cannot grasp the universal. The particulars which arise out of phantasms are perceived by our senses and means of intellectual operation, the human intellectual Cognition takes place. Here the obvious question may arise; how then is the transition from sensitive and particular knowledge to intellectual Cognition effected? The rational soul cannot be effected by a material thing or by the phantasm. Therefore, an activity in the part of soul is needed, since the concept cannot be formed simply passively. This activity is the activity of the Active intellect which illumines the phantasm, and abstracts from it the universal or intelligible species. St. Thomas thus speaks of illumination, but he does not use the word in the full Augustinian sense; he means that Active intellect by its natural power and without any special illumination from God renders visible the intelligible aspect of the phantasm, reveals the universal element contained implicitly in the phantasm. The function of the Active intellect is purely active, to abstract the universal element from the particulars. Here Thomas claimed that the intellect of man contains no innate-ideas but is in potentiality to the reception of concepts.[31] This above statement, indirectly suggests that how Aquinas, if not directly, indirectly at least admits of an innate potentiality of the mind. The terms 'to abstract' means 'to isolate intellectually the universal apart from the particularising notes,' amply suggests also the capacity of the mind, which aims at innate possession, because this cannot be gained from sense perception. Here we find the influence of Augustine over Aquinas so far as his notion of act in the intellect is concerned. In Augustine that was the Divine illumination or a flash of light from the Divine, while in Aquinas it appears as an intellectual light. Therefore, to say that Augustine was wrong in postulating a special Divine illumination and Thomas was right in denying the necessity of such an illumination is an understandable attitude.

Once again Thomas held that the human mind is originally in potentially to knowledge; but it has no innate-ideas. But he continued further that the only sense in which ideas are innate is that the mind has a natural capacity for abstracting and forming ideas : as far as actual ideas go, the mind is originally a *tabula rasa.*[32] This statement clearly justifies that the influence of Aristotle over Aquinas was not final. Because, so far he was in the Aristotelian tradition, he was of the opinion that the mind has no innate-ideas and it is originally a *tabula rasa* (i.e. a clean state, nothing written upon it), but it is clearly revealed from the above statement that in some sense he also accepted the principle of innatism, that is to say, mind has innate natural capacities.

Thomas was of the opinion that the source of minds' knowledge is sense-perception. Even knowledge of the soul is not an exception to this rule. From this it follows then that the human mind cannot in this life attain a direct knowledge of immaterial substances, which cannot be the object of senses. To put it otherwise, the human mind can rise above the things of sense and attain knowledge of God. To this, Thomas reply would be to recall his doctrine of the intellect as such. His explanation is that the senses are determined to one particular kind of objects, but the intellect, being immaterial is the faculty of apprehending being. The intellect as such is directed towards all being, he also accepted that it can proceed beyond senses not being confined to material essences. He continued further and said that, as the mind is a *tabula rasa*, the intellect cannot by its own power apprehend God directly, rather it is sense which reveals the relation to God. First he used to accept that the senses are determined to one particular kind of objects, while the intellect to immaterial beings like God. If this is so, then the individual sense-perception cannot reveal the relation to God which is immaterial being. Hence, it seems that the intellect has got its innate capacity to know God and then it reveals the knowledge of God through senses. Therefore, the notion that the mind is a *tabula Rasa* becomes inappropriate to the philosophy of Aquinas. To substantiate this point further, we can see, that it is a constant conviction of Aquinas that the mind does not start off with any stock of innate-ideas or of innate-knowledge. There, he reaffirms Aristotle's statement that the mind is initially a *tabula rasa* on which nothing has yet been written, "this is clear from the fact that in the beginning we understand only potentially, though after-words we understand actually" (S.Th., 1a 79, 2). To put it otherwise; the mind from the beginning has a capacity for knowing things. The minds' capacity for knowing things does not of course entail the conclusion that it starts its life with a stock of innate-ideas or inborn knowledge. But, does it support the statement that the mind is a *tabula rasa* ? This controversial situation atleast makes one point clear, namely that the re-affirmation of the notion of *tabula ras a* in the case of Aquinas is seem to be incoherent but regarding the doctrine of innate-ideas and its acceptance, indirectly comes from all his assumptions.

Let us see how Thomas analysed his notion of intellect, According to him the intellect is not one faculty but two or a single faculty with two powers;

1. Agent intellect (intellectus agens)
2. Receptive intellect (intellectus possibilis)

Thomas took the concept of the Agent-intellect from Aristotle. Thomas said, to Plato there was no need of Agent intellect, since he believed that the forms of material things subsisted without matter and were thus fit objects of understanding, being immaterial species or ideas. But to Aristotle, there are no forms of things in nature subsisting without matter, and forms existing in matter are not actually intelligible. Therefore Aquinas said the nature of forms of perceptible things which we understand need to be made actually intelligible, which has been done by Agent intellect by abstracting species from material conditions. In contrast to the Active-intellect, there is a receptive-intellect. The respective-intellect is the power to exercise the dispositions acquired by the use of the Agent-intellect. "One and the same soul" we are told, "in so far as it is actually immaterial, has a power called the Agent-intellect which is a power to make other things actually immaterial by abstracting from the conditions of individual matter, and another power to receive ideas of this kind, which is called the receptive intellect as having the power to receive such ideas", (S.Th. Ia 79, 4 ad 4). The receptive-intellect is the *locus of species,* the storehouse of ideas (S.Th.Ia 79, 6 esp. ad 1). Later Aquinas praises Aristotle for taking a middle course between the innate-idealism of Plato and the crude empiricism of Democritus. Aristotle maintained that the intellect had an activity in which the body had no share. Now we see, that nothing corporeal can cause an impression on an incorporeal being, and therefore according to Aristotle the mere stimulus of sensible bodies is not sufficient to cause intellectual activity. Something nobler and higher is needed, which he called the Agent intellect: It makes the phantasms received from the senses to be actually intelligible by means of a certain abstraction (S.Th.Ia 84, 6). Here the obvious question may arise: in what sense these concepts are abstracted from phantasms ? The explanation is that concepts and experiences stand in a certain causal relation, also they stand in a certain formal relation. In this way intellectual activity is caused by the senses on the side of phantasms. But since phantasms are not sufficient to affect the receptive intellect unless they are made actually intelligible by the Agent intellect, sense-knowledge cannot be said to be the total and complete cause of intellectual knowledge. Even thomas contrasts the abstraction made by the intellect with that made by senses. Sense faculties do receive the forms of senseperceptible things without their matter, as it receives the colour of gold, without the gold. Similarly the intellect receives the ideas of bodies, which are material and changeable in an immaterial and unchangeable way of its own (S.Th. Ia 84, 1). Thus the intellect, which abstracts the ideas not only from matter but also from material individuating characteristics, is a more perfect cognitive power than the senses. Therefore the intellect, not only is directly capable of knowing universals but indirectly by a kind of reflection, it can know individuals. Here it is amply justified that it is only through the intellect that we do acquire knowledge proper, not through the sense-perception. This clearly reveals in a way the rationalistic trend in the philosophy of Aquinas and his affinity to Plato and Augustine. To substantiate this in more detail, we find that Thomas Aquinas criticized the conception of innate-ideas of both Plato and in an other way of Augustine, but

Advocates further that, the human intellect possesses a light just sufficient to acquire the knowledge of the intelligibles to which it can raise itself by means of sensible things. He admitted that in a certain sense, indeed, we possess in us the germ of all knowledge : ***Praleexistunt in nobis quaedam Scientiarum Semina.***[33] This statement justify his acceptance of innate-possession of knowledge. Even in the extreme case, if we proceed to the Transcendental Thomism, it is claimed there also that the whole metaphysics is virtually inborn in man.[34]

The theory of knowledge of Thomas would be incomplete, if his ethics is not discussed here. In ethics, he categorically mentioned that the tendencies of man's nature are innate but the knowledge of how to rectify their inclinations stems from the natural use of man's understanding.[35]

Therefore he advocates that the natural light of reason by which we discern what is good and what is evil which is the function of the natural law, is nothing else than an imprint of us of the Divine light. It is therefore evident that the natural law is nothing else than the natural creatures' participation in the eternal laws.[36] The notion of innatism which was implicitly there in the philosophy of Aquinas now becomes prominent. when he confirmed that what is given to man at birth is not a code of moral laws but simply the power of intellect. Therefore, he admitted that what is innate in us is not actual knowledge that God exists, but the natural light of reason and its principles.[37]

Hence, it is found that, Thomas Aquinas played an important role in bringing the gap between Ancient and Modern philosophy. His analysis of knowledge seems quite similar to that of Kant. Like Kant, he emphasises the sensible origin of intellectual knowledge and like Kant, he is aware that intellectual activity is different from sense-perception. Therefore intellectual Aquinas was in the line of Kant's famous statement that, "But though all our knowledge begins with experience, it does not follow that it all arises out of experience."[38] (B1)

(iv) Conclusion

To Plato, the soul understands corporeal things through innate-species. In St. Augustine, also we have seen how he has been influenced by the Platonic tradition and accepted the doctrine of innate ideas, if not completely in the Platonic way but in some other manner. For Plato, the soul understands through an innate species and for Augustine it is because of Divine illumination. In St. Bonaventure, we find a projection of St. Augustine's philosophy, clearly admitting the doctrine in the form of Divine illumination. On the contrary, Thomas Aquinas maintained that soul does not know corporeal things through innate-species. This happened in the case of Aquinas, because of the influence of Aristotle over him, but I have already given an elaborate exposition, to show that the influence of Aristotle over Aquinas was not an exclusive one, rather Aquinas was also a product of both Platonic and Augustenian tradition.

Regarding the contribution to the doctrine of innate-ideas from the Ancient to Medieval period, we find that the crude and passive form of innate-ideas of Plato appears in St. Augustine in the form of an illumination, which pre-supposes a Divine act. The notion of Divine act which indirectly resembles the doctrine of innate-ideas, gives a new life to the doctrine. To put it otherwise, the passivity attached to the doctrine becomes an active element. The theological interpretation of the doctrine gets itself purifield in St. Bonaventure, when he demonstrated the illumination having some form of empirical origin. So his epistemology became complex because it brings together both Aristotelian and Platonic elements. When we came to Thomas Aquinas, we find that he was struggling hard to disect the vital concepts from their theological interpretations. As an indication to this we find, how Thomas gradually eliminated some absurdities attached to the doctrine of innate-ideas but only assumed the power of intellect in the form of the natural light of reason. With this sort of modification, he was successful in bringing the concept nearer to modern philosophy.

REFERENCES

1. Cf., Armstrong, A. H., edited, *The Cambridge History of Later Greek and Early Medieval Philosophy*. (Cambridge, at the University Press 1967) pp. 364-65.

2. E. Gilson, *History of Christian Philosophy in the Middle Ages*, (Sheed and Ward, London: 1955) pp. 75-76.
3. M. Wulf., *History of Medieval Philosophy*, Vol. I, (Thomas Nelson and Sons, 1952) p. 84.
4. E. Gilson, *The Christian Philosophy of St. Augustine*, (Victor Gollancz Ltd., London: 1961) p. 76.
5. Ibid., p. 82.
6. Ibid., p. 91.
7. Op. Cit., A. H. Armstrong, p. 370.
8. F. Copleston, *A History of Medieval Philosophy*, (Methuen and Co., 1972) p. 35.
9. Ibid., p. 94.
10. Op. Cit., E. Gilson, *History of Christian Philosophy in the Middle Ages*, p. 75.
11. Op. Cit., M. Wulf, p. 84. (Note)
12. Op. Cit., E. Gilson, p. 71.
13. For instance—De civit. Dei., X, 2.
14. Paul, Edwards, *The Encyclopaedia of Philosophy*, Vol. 4 (Macmillan Company and the Free Press, 1967).
15. E. Gilson, *The Philosophy of St. Bonaventure*, (Sheed and Ward: 1938) Chapter, xii.
16. For further study please refer, Op. cit., Gilson, *History of Christian Philosophy in the Middle Ages*, ff. 331.
17. Op. Cit., F. C. Copleston, *History of Medieval Philosophy*, p. 163.
18. Ibid., p. 164.
19. S. J. Curtis, *A Short History of Western Philosophy in the Middle Ages*, (Macdonald and Co., (Publishers) Ltd., London: 1950) p. 205.
20. Cf. Op. cit., *History of Medieval Philosophy*, F. C. Copleston, p. 166.
21. Cf. Op. cit. *A Short History of Western Philosophy in the Middle Ages*, p. 208.
22. Cf. David Knowles, *The Evolution of Medieval Thought*, (Longman, London: 1970) p. 246.
23. Cf. F. C. Copleston, *Aquinas*, (Penguin Books) 1970, pp. 27-28.
24. Cf. Op. cit., F. C. Copleston, *A History of Medieval Philosophy*, p. 180.
25. J. Maritain, *The Degrees of Knowledge*, (Geoffrey Bles, London: 1959) p. 292.
26. Ibid., pp. 302-3.
27. Cf. A. Kenny., edited, Aquinas: *A Collection of Critical Essays*, (Macmillan, 1969) p. 1.
28. Op. Cit., Maritain, p. 306.
29. Ibid., p. 306.
30. Cf. Op. cit., Curtis, *A Short History of Wastern Philosophy in the Middle Ages*, p. 136.
31. F. Copleston, *A History of Philosophy*, Vol. II (Burns Oates and Washbourne Ltd., London: 1950) p. 390.

32. Cf. Op. cit., F. Copleston, *A History of Philosophy*, Vol. II, p. 392.
33. De. Veritate, XI, 1. (Cf. Gilson, *The Christian Philosophy of St. Thomas Aquinas*) p. 472.
34. Cf. *The Monist*: January 1974, "Transcendental Thomism" by J. Doncell, S. J.
35. Cf. *The Monist*, January 1974, Vol. 58, No. 1, "*Is Thomas Aquinas a Natural Law Ethicist*", by Vernon J. Bourke.
36. S. Th. 1-11, q. 91, a. 2.
37. Cf. Gilson, *The Christian Philosophy of St. Thomas Aquinas* (Victor Gollancz Ltd., London: 1961) p. 55.
38. N. K. Smith, *Kant's Critique of Pure Reason*, (Macmillan & Co., London: 1961).

Note: Appendix-A, may please be referred for further discussions regarding the affinity between St. Augustine's theory of Divine illumination and St. Thomas Aquinas's Notion of Agent intellect, which also includes the debate, '*Whether Agent intellect forms a part of the soul or not.*'

3

Some Aspects of the Renaissance Conception of Mind and Nature

(i) Renaissance Humanism

The period of Renaissance, which I shall discuss here, can be identified from about the middle of the 14th century to the end of the 17th century. This period had witnessed a considerable change in the fields of art, literature, science and classical learning. The philosophical literature of the Renaissance is in fact rich and diversified, because it had extended its discussion to almost all fields of intellectual concern. While discussing the Renaissance philosophy, one has to centre around the thinkers of Italy, as Italy held a dominating place in the field of culture during that period.

My main concern would be here to explore the epistemological assumptions of the Renaissance and how they have contributed a surprisingly modern outlook to that. The epistemology of Ancient and Medieval period which I have already discussed in the preceding chapters in connection with the central concept of innateness, is now being modified and a sudden change is brought about by the Renaissance thinkers, particularly by the Scientific Renaissance. The important concern of ours would be to study how this transformation of the problem of knowledge from the theological level to the level of a problem of Philosophy of Science took place. Generally, we can see how the general problem of epistemology changed to a secular form of epistemology, which features prominently in the philosophy of Descartes, Locke, etc. Further, I would discuss how the religious man of Antiquity and Medieval period appeared as a secular being in the philosophy of Renaissance and how the search for the dignity of man became a burning issue, which culminated in the philosophy of science.

While discussing the philosophy of Renaissance, I would divide them broadly earlier and latter periods. In the earlier part, I would concentrate on Humanism, Revival of Platonism and Revival of Aristotelianism. In the latter part, it would be the discussion of the Renaissance philosophy of Nature and Scientific Renaissance. While discussing these parts, I would simply represent their views through the dominant representative of that period with some reference to others, if necessary.

In Italy towards the end of 13th century, Petrarca was considered as '*father of Humanism*; again he was followed by a number of humanists during the rest of the period influenced by the cultural life of Italy. The primary concern of Humanism was to deal with the cultural and educational ideal of the Humanists based on the study of Classical Greek and Latin authors. The Humanist movement with the Classicism it brought about was the most pervasive element of the Renaissance Culture. The *literary* works of Humanists makes it clear that their interest in philosophy was secondary and was limited to Ethics. In spite of such secondary interest, they influenced the style and the form of philosophical literature and they also made available a number of Ancient philosophical texts not known to the Middle ages; in this way they were the cause of revival of other Ancient philosophies besides Aristotelianism.

Between Plato and Aristotle, the humanists rejected Aristotle, because of his scientific interest; rather they were in agreement with Plato, for their intellectual interest, because they were at bottom primarily religious. Therefore, Patrarca launched a strong attack against the contemporary Averroistic Aristotelians. The main concern of Petrarca, which became emphatic in Ficino and Pico, was the search for the dignity of man. It was in fact in his philosophy that the idea of secular man germinated and latter on had its full growth in the entire Renaissance. Humanism which brought to the Western world a large body of secular learning and literature, that was neither religious nor scientific or professional.

(ii) Renaissance Platonism

Platonism was the most imposing alternative to the Aristotelian schools because of its religious values, which linked it to the values of human life. Platonism had already been thoroughly Christianised by the Augustinian tradition, which had dominated the Medieval thought and also retained its strength thereafter with a Christianised Aristotelianism.

Marsilio Ficino, was a most influential exponent of Platonism in Italy during 15th century. He devoted himself to the task of reviving Platonism. For Ficino, Augustine became the guide in judging Platonism to be superior than other philosophies. This conviction of Ficino made him the leader of the Platonic Academy of Florence, which became the most important centre of Platonic influence in Western Europe. Ficino tried to summarise the metaphysical doctrines in his major work the *Theologia Platonica,* where he developed the doctrine of the dignity of man and the immortality of the soul. Ficino's Platonism was in many ways a product of the Humanistic movement. Yet, Ficino was more than a mere humanist who happened to be interested in Plato. He was very much attracted by the thought of Plato and neo-Platonism. Consequently he was not, like most humanists, opposed to the traditions of the Medieval schools but was strongly influenced by them. Therefore, we find the influence of Platonism in the Renaissance was much deeper than that of the Humanistic movement. It not only transmitted the works of Plato, through Plotinus and other Ancient thinkers, it also gave a new interpretation to the Platonic and neo-Platonic doctrines which showed originality in many points.

His insistance on the immortality of soul demonstrated, that the basic phenomenon of human life is the inward experience of Contemplation which culminates in the immediate vision and enjoyment of God. Since this immediate vision is attained on earth by a few, for a brief moment, we must postulate a future life in which the goal of human existence will be attained, otherwise the whole of human life would lose its meaning. And unless that human mind somehow possessed the excellence of infinity and eternity in itself, it could not incline towards an infinite end. Here the Platonic element of Ficino is clearly visible, which ultimately was expressed in his theory of knowledge.

Ficino's theory of knowledge was in the line of St. Augustine which was completely Platonic in trend. His acceptance of the immortality of the soul justified that, all knowledge comes from God acting within the soul. God working through this innate sense of harmony reveals his infinity immortal ideas. Like Plato, Ficino even advocated that the rational soul is more perfect than the senses and the intellect superior to that of sense. He explained further that sense has no power to know either itself or intellect and the object of intellect. All these remains for intellect to be known. By reason only we decide which is more perfect. Because this power enquires by reasoning and assigns a reason for its decision, it is reason, not the sense. Therefore, *intellect* alone is that which knows all things.

An intellect is more *perfect* than sense, man is more perfect than the brutes and by means of that intelligence, the human being approaches God through love and worship. The attainment of this end becomes easier in proportion to the *richness* of the innate perfection of that thing; because the formal perfection which is innate from the beginning is stranger. Only for this, the reason can attain the end easily than sense.[1] This analysis presupposes that, for Ficino, intellect and its functions, which are superior to that of senses, is innately there in the human mind and helps in the construction of knowledge.

Ficino's insistent approach of reason being superior than senses, simply demonstrated his acceptance of the Platonic theory of knowledge of the *Meno* and the *Phaedo*, which I have discussed in other places. In support of this view, Randall, in his book rightly remarks, "Ficino's Augustinian theory of knowledge, stripped of the Aristotelian psychology with which the Middle Ages had provided it, and buttressed from the *Meno* and the *Phaedo*. All knowledge is from innate formulae in the mind, which, stimulated by sense objects, recall the divine ideas. Not by abstraction from particulars, for how could a mere heap generate a single simple concept?—but by Divine illumination."[2]

The above passage clearly indicates that Ficino was a close follower of both Plato and St. Augustine. Their influence was so deep in him, that even the predominant trend of Aristotelianism could not make any fundamental change in his views.

(iii) Renaissance Aristotelianism

The third philosophical current of the Itallian Renaissance was the humanistic Aristotelianism of Pompanazzi and Zabralla. The Aristotelianism with the central concern for the field of logic and method, natural philosophy and metaphysics made its appearance towards the end of 13th century.

Pompanazzi, like Ficino, focused attention on man and his destiny. Both emphasized individual and personal values, in this both were humanists. But while Ficino and Platonists went back to Hellinistic world of religious philosophies of Alexandria, the naturalistic humanism of Pompanazzi and Zabralla was built on the traditions of Italian Aristotelianism and original philosophy towards natural science.

The most important work of Pompanazzi was on immortality of soul, that was mainly a reply to Ficino, where Pompanazzi explained his views regarding soul and its immortality. For Pompanazzi soul is absolutely mortal, and only relatively immortal. His contention was that there is no possibility of direct insight of a spiritual character, since all knowledge is based on sense. The end of human life is moral virtue, which can be attained by every human being during his earthly existence. Hence, there is no rational necessity of the immortality of soul. Even in other writings he asserted that the immortality of soul is rather a neutral problem.

It was only because of Aristotelian influence that Pompanazzi differred on the issue of immortality of soul with Ficino, but regarding the issue of dignity of Man both share same views, Ficino's conception of Man is simply echoed by Pompanazzi. While discussing Pompanazzi, I will not explain his Aristotelian attitude, rather I would concentrate, how he shaped the subject matter of philosophy distinct from theology which would contribute substantially to the Natural and Scientific Renaissance of the latter period.

The Aristotelianism of Pompanazzi maintained a secular *rationalism*, which kept philosophy independent of theology without interpreting its dogmatic teachings. This novel treatment dramatically changed the subject-matter of philosophy and lead towards a natural and scientific approach. While giving this novel idea, Pompanazzi glorified the dignity of Man, which was one of the favourite themes of the early Renaissance. But later on it produced a strong reaction because in the Italian schools the science of Nature emerged as a prominent concern. This does not mean that there was a break of theological interest, rather it came as a sustained and collective criticism of Aristotelian ideas. The mathematical and mechanical development at the end of 16th century produced by Galileo, owes very little to the Platonic revival but received a powerful response from the Critical Aristotelians of the Italian Universities. Therefore, the clear separation between philosophy and theology, which was initiated by Pompanazzi could not arrive at a purely naturalistic or anti-religious position, rather it paved the way for later Western Thought. One can very well visualize the work of Pompanazzi, the way he established the relation between earlier and later period of the Renaissance. The main contribution of Pompanazzi was to give a secular interpretation of both man and philosophy, which ultimately was done by Galileo.

(iv) **Renaissance Philosophers of Nature**

The pioneers of this current roughly include Telesio. Patrizi and Bruno. The main interest of these men were in natural philosophy and cosmology. They tried to formulate a novel thesis and were proud to free themselves from the Ancient philosophical authorities, especially from Aristotle, who had dominated philosophical speculation, particularly Natural philosophy.

Starting from Antiquity, if one wants to unravel the philosophy in general and problem of knowledge in particular, one would not find any concrete suggestion given by any school of thought, rather all moved in their own world of discourse without accepting views of others. One reason of this desperate situation may be of theological superstition which was ruling over the entire philosophical world. Not even a single system, school or individual thinker was away from this theological traditional believes. But as the modern man became aware of his own surroundings he started thinking in terms of eliminating the prevailing circumstances, and to give something original not at the risk of Ancient doctrines but with some modern outlook. This trend has been initiated generally by these Renaissance philosophers of Nature. They were of opinion that one can have new discoveries to attain knowledge that had not been accessible to the Ancients. This determination actually witnessed the first tangible advances achieved beyond the reach of Ancients, in the fields of mathematics and astronomy, anatomy and botany.

Inspite of their conviction, they could not able to dissociate themselves completely from the influence of Plato and Aristotle, yet the attitude remains significant. For this independedt outlook they were hailed as forerunners of Modern speculative philosophy of science. Their endeavour extinguished by this steady and successful progress of the Natural and other sciences.

If an account of this short lived group of Renaissance would be given, we find they all differ not only in their opinion but also in their structure and orientation of thought.

Telesio, in broad sense belongs to Aristotelian tradition. For him knowledge can be reduced to sense-perception. Even he attempted to derive reason and its universal concepts from sensation. He may even be considered as direct or indirect forerunner of Newton and Locke.

Patrizi, another exponent of that period was not in Aristotelian tradition like Telesio, rather he can be grouped with Platonists than with Aristotelians. One distinct point of his being Platonic and anti-Aristotletian was his interest of Mathematics. In his opinion, Platonic philosophy gives a very high status and a great importance to mathematical knowledge. So far as his theory of knowledge is concerned, he followed Plato and demonstrated that "all knowledge is occasioned by sense, but its origin is in the mind."[3] Because of his rationalistic attitude he criticized sensualism of Telesio, one of his contemporaries.

The sensualism and empiricism of Telesio and the Neo-Platonism of Patrizi were merged in the thought of Campanella, a pupil of Telesio. He had a very poor opinion of mathematics which he founded on his empirical theory rather than on his Platonism. According to his opinion, Mathematics, like Logic, fails to grasp the full reality of a particular thing.

Bruno was the most important exponent of this period. He restates the Copernican system of the Universe and gives to it for the first time a particular meaning. He not only adopted the Copernican system but also boldly discarded such time honoured notions as the radical distinction between celestical and earthly things and the hierarchical view of Nature. Being aware of his novel views, he did not spare Aristotle and his followers. Therefore, it has been rightly remarked that he was a forerunner but not a founder of Modern science and philosophy. He was unaware of the role that mathematics and experimental observation were to play in Modern science. Therefore, he could not develop a precise method by which his assertions might have been demonstrated.

In spite of their difference of opinion, philosophers of Nature occupy a prominent place in the Renaissance for their intrinsic quality of their contribution to Modern science and its philosophy. The reason for their separation from Modern scientists was their failure to find a firm and valid method of natural inquiry and especially to appreciate the fundamental importance of mathematics. Therefore, the Aristotelian tradition of Natural philosophy could not be overthrown by the outside attacks of Humanists or Platonists nor by the suggestive theories of the Natural Philosophers. It yielded in only after the 17th century, when the new science of Galileo, dealt with the subject-matter on the basis of a firmly established and *superior method.*

If we attempt to sum up the visions of all Natural philosophers, we may conclude that for them, man and nature are similar, that man is through and through natural and nature is human. But the new science later on claimed sharply, to insist that nature is not human but mathematical and mechanical and that man lives as a kingdom within nature.

All the above notions gave a very strong impetus to Modern science to carry out its programme. When we speak of Modern science we are thinking primarily of the mathematical physics of Galileo, which started toward the last year of the 16th century. Galileo, the founder of Modern science, was in many ways indebted to the Renaissance.

With the re-constructed method of mathematical analysis and demonstration, the scientists went forward to explore nature's secrets. They revolutionized man's conception of the Universe. The revolution in the cosmology involved two fundamental changes, one associated with Copernicus and the other with Galileo. It remains for Bruno and Kepler to express the philosophical significance of what Copernicus had done and on the other hand to Descartes and Spinoza to carry out Galileo's suggested picture.

(v) Scientific Renaissance

Copernicus

Copernicus was responsible for the revival of mathematics. He approached the problems primarily as a mathematician and Scientist with little philosophical interest. Kepler and Bruno, two naturalistic neo-Platonists of the Renaissance gave philosophical interpretation to theories and method of Copernicus. Of Bruno and Kepler, it was Kepler who made him a philocophical scientist rather than a metaphysician and founder of new humanistic religion. Kepler had become a Platonist following genuine mathematics. It was he, who worked out the first philosophical analysis of Modern science.

This fundamental concept of mathematical relation is embedded in the traditional Platonic view of knowledge. Even in the *Optics*, Kepler developed the Platonic theory and Augustinian theory of perception to account for the mixture of sense and geometry in vision. The Platonic foundation, make Kepler to advocate that perfect and eertain knowledge is always mathematical. He further explained that the knowledge of quantities is innate in the soul and determines of what kind the eye must be. The structure of the eye follows the nature of the intellect, not *vice-versa*. Just the eye was made to see colours, and the ear to hear the sounds, so the human mind was made to understand, not whatever you please, but quantity[4] only.

Kepler

It is this conviction about the mathematical *character* of the world and this necessarily mathematical character of human knowledge that makes Kepler to break away from the Medieval tradition. Kepler was clearly aware of his differences with Aristotle in his mathematical convictions. Quantity is the primary accident of the substance, prior to the other Categories. Aristotle explained nature in terms of qualitative categories and therefore left mathematics in an intermediate position. The Orthodox Aristotelian school minimized the importance of mathematics. Mathematics was assigned an intermediate dignity between metaphysics and physics. Nature was fundamentally qualitative. The key to the highest knowledge must therefore, *be logic rather than mathematics*. But on the other hand Kepler found himself quantitative proportions in all things to elevate mathematics to the highest point. He concluded that all certain knowledge must be knowledge of their quantitative characteristics. Perfect knowledge is always mathematical and further he claimed that the conclusions of mathematics are most certain and indubitable. Without mathematics even the eye of the mystic is blind.[5]

Kepler was entirely convinced on *a priori* grounds that the universe is basically mathematical. and that all genuine knowledge must be mathematical, but he made it plain that the laws of thought are innate in us as a Divine gift, and cannot come to any knowledge of themselves; there must be the perceived motions which furnish the material for their exact exemplification.[6]

Thus to Kepler the real world is mathematical harmony discoverable in things. The changeable surface qualities which do not fit into this underlying harmony are on a lower level of reality. They do not so truly exist. This trend of thought influenced Kepler deeply because of his acceptance to Copernican theory, because the movement of earth increased the distrust of the senses and experience, and consequently mathematics is considered as the only source of unshakable knowledge.

The reason why there exists this vast and beautiful mathematical order in the universe is not further explicable for Kepler except by way of his neo-Platonism. Kepler said in approval of Plato, that God ever geometrizes; he created the world in accordance with numerical harmonies,[7] and that is why he made the human mind such that it can only know by quantity. This mathematical expedition of Kepler reached its climax in Galileo and transformed the world into a mathematical machine.

Galileo

The main work of Galileo was to replace, qualitative physics of Aristotle with quantitative mathematical physics. Whether Plato's authority was used in this connection, is not too certain, and would have to be further explored.[8] Inspite of that Galileo's original contribution was considered to be novel.

Aristotle drew a sharp distinction between mathematics and Physics, the later is less abstract, less removed from matter and motion than the former. Physics tells us what sort of being there are in the world around us. Mathematics is the science of quantified things, considering only the quantitative aspects. Quantity only tells us how much of the element we had not, the kind of essence. The language of Physics is thus directly drawn from the concrete perceptual qualitative terms of everyday use.

This approach to Physics gradually began to be modified under the pressure of Platonists' success. The way was prepared by Galileo's famous dictum '*the book of nature is written in the language of mathematics.*' This represented the *entire* abandonment of Aristotelian non-mathematical physics. Galileo made the necessary distinction between mathematics as a language or syntax and mathematics as a locus of truth about some subject matter. By doing so he was not returning to the Plantonism of the *Timaeus*, where the physicist had to look to the mathematician not only for his language but for the evidence he needed about the nature of the physical universe. When Plato says that the Universe is composed of atoms of certain shapes, the warrant he urges for his claim comes not from physics not from observation but from geometry. The basic inadequacy of the Platonic view is therefore to be seen in a failure to integrate the mathematical and the empirical components of scientific knowledge. The emphasis upon the necessity of mathematics for scientific knowledge was the valid contribution of Platonism. But this emphasis without a correlative theory of the role of experience makes the final picture again inadequate. At the practical level Galileo's achievement is to effect this synthesis between mathematics and observation. This practical synthesis was sufficient for the strictly scientific revolution which he brought about. But the practical synthesis has to be formulated at the epistemological level also as a theory of the scientific method which will integrate theoretically the rational and the empirical components of knowledge. This theoretical aspect of the thesis was suggested by Galileo but not be satisfactorily solved by him. It became therefore one of the fundamental problems of philosophers after the Renaissance and it reached a provisional solution in the critical philosophy of Kant.

While criticizing Aristotelian qualitative physics and logical methodology, Galileo advocated that: "Logic teaches us to know, whether the conclusions and demonstrations which are already discovered and at hand are consistent, but it cannot be said that it teaches us how to find consistent conclusions and demonstrations."[9] We do not learn them from Logic, but from the books which are full of demonstrations which are the mathematical not the logical.[10]

This method of mathematical demonstration being grounded in the structure of nature, is independent of sensible verification. Rather this is an exclusively *a priori* method of reaching at truth. Therefore, in Galileo we find a realization of mathematical interpretation of nature, because for him Nature is the domain of mathematics. Galileo puts it very clearly in one of his famous writings: "Philosophy is written in this grand book, the Universe, which stands continually open to our gaze. But the book cannot be understood unless one first learns to understand the language and to know the letters in which it is written." He continued further: "It is written in language of mathematics, and the letters are triangles, circles, and other geometrical figures, without which it is humanly impossible to understand a single word."[11]

This above trend of thought clearly indicates the innate dispositions of the human being to understand the world of Nature. Because whatever can be said of Nature in mathematical discourre is truly said, and the structure it grasps God himself could have no clearer knowledge.

While explaining his mathematical interpretation of Nature, he adopted the view that his propositions can be demonstrated mathematically but confirmed by experiment. Galileo proceeds further that sense-experience should not be in conflict with truth. But that sense must be accompanied by *discorso*, by reason. For reason is the test of experience. And that *discorso* must be mathematical.[12] Therefore, Galileo combined both mathematical and experimental methods in science. Galileo, in order to explain his point further, stated that it is clear that philosophy wants to explain what is revealed by senses. But the world of senses is not its own explanation; it is a book written in strange language, which has to be interpreted in the alphabets of that language, that alphabets are the principles and units of mathematics. On the one hand, we cannot deny that it is the senses which offer us the world to be explained; on the other hand, we are equally certain that they don't give us the rational order which alone supplies the desired explanation. The latter is always mathematical and it is possible only by mathematical demonstration. The Kantian role played by Galileo here was being overlooked but the fact remained that both had the same trend of thought.

Like Kepler, Galileo also explained that this mathematical interpretation of nature must be in exact terms, should not be with vague Pythagorian mysticism. Therefore, in his greatest work the *Mathematical Demonstrations of Two New Branches of Science*, he reveals himself as the follower, not of Pythagoras but of Archimedes.[13]

Galileo explained himself further by dividing knowledge into extensive and intensive or knowing can be undertaken intensively and extensively. Knowing intensively means, knowing perfectly any proposition, such as that of pure-mathematical sciences, of which the Divine intellect knows indeed infinitely more propositions, since it knows them all. Whatever we know by mathematical demonstrations is the very constitution and structure of things. Because mathematics best expresses the natural structure of things.

It was this absolute confidence in mathematics as the language by which the structure of the world can be grasped, best amplified the existence of innate notions of human mind irrespective of the collective opposition. And this conviction of Galileo sustained him further in his conflict with the Church.

This mathematization of Nature is carried further to its limit by Descartes during his period but that has been challenged by Newton. However, both had this much in common, that the book of nature is written in the Language of mathematics and to understand that nature, the human mind should possess innate dispositions.

(vi) Conclusion

Here I will simply give a brief account of the Renaissance period, so far as their achievements and consequences are concerned.

Achievements

The achievements of the Renaissance period in general and of philosophy in particular were quite substantial. The conviction that, one can entirely dissociate himself from the traditional dogmatic believes, has been successfully drafted by the Renaissance thinkers. In this connection their moral contribution to philosophy were the secularization of the epistemology and mathematical interpretation of nature. So far as the former is concerned, il emerged from the philosophy of Humanistic Renaissance and carried on further successfully, changed the entire conception of Man and the Philosophy he is concerned with. This independent nature of man made him free from the clutches of Ancient and dogmatic believes. Finally it is revealed that man can think of himself and the nature around him independent of theological interpretations. As a consequence to this we find the mathematical interpretation of nature and assumptions for secular epistemology. Mathematics which has become a vital instrument to disect the nature with the Renaissance thinkers, was of course a borrowed notion but the fact remains that this aspect has been overlooked by Ancients and Medievals. Galileo very successfully employed mathematics to reveal the secrets of the nature, and concluded that it is possible, because the human mind is supplied with innate mathematical knowledge.

Consequences

As the achievements were glaring similarly the questions they posed for the future philosophers were surprisingly vital.

It is revealed from the previous explanation that the Renaissance period literally revolutionized the entire field of speculative philosophy. But they could not supply any conclusive answer to their epistemological assumptions, rather it seems that they demonstrated the skeleton without adding any flesh to that. One can substantiate this point discussing Galileo's claims for innate mathematical knowledge and its validation in sense-experience. Galileo opined that his propositions can be demonstrated mathematically and confirmed by experience and claimed further that the sense-experience should be accompanied by reason which is the test of experience. This point of Galileo suggests working out the epistemological connections between the innate mathematical ideas and their validation in sense-experience. Granted that there are innate-mathematical ideas, once again granted that their validation depends in sense-experience, but how the relation would be established in order to deliver the knowledge was not explicitly demonstrated by Galileo. That task remained particularly for Kant to be done at a later stage. In this sense the Renaissance has prepared the Kantian question. Galileo displayed the quantitative physics and demonstrated the existence of mathematical knowledge of nature. A further epistemological problem was to explain the possibility of such knowledge has not been dealt by him. This task is essentially done by Modern philosophers, particularly by Kant.

This mathematical interpretation of nature further suggests the task of working out a conception of mind as the source of innate knowledge. The nature of mind and soul need further analysis so as to give a basis to the new type of epistemology. So far the Renaissance had only supplied the view that the mind is capable of inner-dispositions but never made any concrete suggestion towards the structure and activities of mind. If we unravel this point further, we find that the Ancients and Medievals claimed the source of innate-ideas either in terms of theology or Divine Illumination. But after careful consideration of Renaissance thinkers, it is found that it is very useful for epistemological analysis. Rather the present situation demands the further task of developing a philosophy of mind. And the same has been explicitly demonstrated in the philosophy of Descartes, Locke and Kant. So far as the source of innate-ideas are concerned the Modern thinkers either positively or negatively contributed their views. Granted that there are innate-ideas, what about the *locus* of such ideas? Descartes made it clear that the mind is such that it has no limitations for innate knowledge. For Locke, the nature of mind is such that nothing is innate but in Kant we find a compromising attitude. Their contribution certainly reveal that innate-knowledge never derived from God and Divine Illumination. The epistemological assumptions of the Renaissance still more suggest, a distinction between innate knowledge and empirical knowledge, which has become an important concern for the immediate future philosophers.

Galileo's mathematical interpretation of nature further suggests that the mind is endowed with innate capacities; granted that the mind possessed that, but what about its nature; has it got innate ideas and innate principles? In other words, are there innate-ideas like substance and innate principles like theory of causation in our knowledge of nature? These are the important queries that emerged out of the Renaissance, for further investigation. Roughly one can conclude that the Renaissance left the task of possibility of scientific knowledge of nature to be further explained by Modern thinkers.

REFERENCES

1. Cassirer, Kristeller, Randal, Jr., edited., *Renaissance Philosophy of Man.*, Phoenix Books, University of Chicago Press, 1956, p. 207.
2. Randall Jr., *The Career of Philosophy*, Vol. I. (Columbia University Press: 1966) p. 58.
3. Cf. Ibid., p. 208.
4. Cf., Ibid., p. 320.
5. Cf., Ibid., p. 322.
6. *Opera*, V, 229 (Cf. *Metaphysical Foundations of Modern Physical Science*, Edwin Arthur Burtt., Routledge & Kegen Paul, London, Reprint, 1950) p. 60.
7. Opera, I, 31 (Cf. *Metaphysical Foundations of Modern Physical*

Science, Edwin Arthur Burtt., Routledge & Kegan Paul, London, Reprint, 1950) p. 58.

8. Cf., Kristeller, *Eight Philosophers of Italian Renaissance*, (Stanford University Press, 1966) p. 118.
9. *Opera*, XIII, 134 (Cf. Op. cit., *Metaphysical Foundations of Modern Physical Science*, Burtt). p. 65.
10. Ibid., 1, 42 (Cf. Ibid., p. 65).
11. Galileo, ed. naz, IV, 171 (Cf. *The making of Modern Science*, edited by, A. Rupert Hall, Leicester University Press, 1960) p. 17.
12. Op. cit., Randall Jr., *Career of Philosophy*, p. 345.
13. Cf. Randall Jr., *The Making of the Modern Mind*, (Houghton Mifflin Company, 1954) p. 238.

4

The Problem of Innateness in Descartes

(i) Innate Ideas : Methodological and Epistemological Considerations

Post-Renaissance period begins with Descartes in whom we find one of the most subtle expositions of the concept of innateness and its role in epistemology. It is essential to study the Cartesian position, because Descartes was the first who successfully carried further the promises of Galileo and very methodically represented his views pertaining the dominant role of innate-ideas in epistemology, keeping mathematics throughout before him. To achieve these logical consequences, Descartes worked out a programme, which I would discuss here, taking his earlier and later works into consideration. While I would undertake to explain his programme, my central concern would be to explore his epistemology as expounded in his later writings, which were already assumed in the unfinished little treatise called the *Regulae* (Rules for the Direction of Mind), because it is natural that one's methodology should proceed in collaboration with one's rules. If we accept the Descartes' major later works the ***Discours on Method*** (Discours de la Method), the *Mediattions* (Meditationes), the ***Principles of Philosophy*** (Principia Philosophiae), contributed to his programme, then it would be rational to conclude that they were implicit in the rules, though not fully, but at least roughly. Let us, hence study the status of the *Regulae*, which has become a controversial issues in the interpretation of philosophy of Descartes.

Charles Adam suggests that the *Regulae ad Directionem Ingenii*, the unfinished dialogue, *La Recherche de la Verite par la Lumiere Maturelle*, and *Le Monde*, are related to *Discours de la Methode*, *Meditationes* and *Principia Philosophiae*, as the first crude sketch for a finished masterpiece.[1] This view is fully confirmed by comparison of the *Regulae* with the *Discours*.

The *Discours* was first published in 1637, as the exposition of the general principles of the Cartesian Method, while, the *Regulae* was written probably in the winter of 1628-29 or even earlier and is unfinished.[2]

The work was to have been complete in 36 rules falling into three parts containing 12 rules each. The first part gives the general nature of Descartes' new Method; while in the second a transition is made to its application in the field of Mathematics. Unfortunately, the treatise, which was never completed, breaks off after Rule XXI, and indeed the explanation of the last three rules is also omitted. The third part was to have shown the application of the method to the general problems of philosophy.[3]

The passage amply demonstrates the immaturity of the work but neverthless, it suggests the programme which is later on found in the other writings of Descartes. Therefore, Joachim has rightly remarked "a detailed study of the *Ragulae* is instructive as well as interesting, if for no other reason than that it constitutes the first material for the examination of the Cartesian conception of *Vera Mathesis*. Though nothing emerges in the *Ragulae* which is irreconcilable with the traditional exposition of the method, yet it presents difficulties which do not appear in the *Discours*, and so provides a fuller understanding of Descartes' teaching."[4] Haldane and Ross clearly mentioned in a note: "Much of the Doctrine contained in this work will be afterwards met with in the '*Method Meditations*', etc., but there are important points in which there is a discrepancy between the earlier and later writings. More noteworthy still is the fact that there are several speculative suggestions (e.g. those about 'Simple Natures') which never received further development in Descartes' Philosophy.[5] Because of the immaturity, it is quite natural to find some discrepancies, but the central tendency seems to have not been contradicted in the later writings. Therefore, A.K. Stout has rightly remarked that: "... though the *Regulae* is earlier than the *Meditations*, there is no evidence in his later writings to show that he had changed his mind."[6] These remarks amply suggest that the influence of the *Ragulae* on other mature later writings of Descartes. To quote Roth: "Considerable discussion has taken place about the relationship between the unfinished *Regulae* and the *Discours*, and the issue has been obscured by the fact that the *Discours* was published some ten years later than the period during which the *Regulae* is usually held to have been composed. The truth would seem to be that it is the second chapter of the *Discours* which represents the earlier draft of the method, as, indeed, the narrative of the *Discours* itself asserts."[7] He continued further that "if we turn to it we see that Descartes singles out Rules 5 to 7 as embodying his central doctrine (the rest of the treatise being only their detailed working out), and a moment's comparison will show that these are identical with the Rules 2, 3, and 4 of the *Discours*. Since the first rule of the *Discours* is implied in Rules 2 and 3 of the *Regulae*, we may take it that the fundamental doctrine of the *Regulae* and the *Discours* is the same. We should not speak then of two stages of Descartes' doctrine of method, and still less of two different doctrines. His primary conception remained unaltered from the earliest times of which we have record, and the rules of the *Discours* are its classic, as they are its earliest, expression."[8] Even S.V. Keeling[9] insists that the *Regulae* throws much more light on the *Method* than the *Discours* does, and the importance of doctrine of Simple Natures which was explicitly mentioned only in the *Ragulae*, suggests its continuity with other writings in spite of its immaturity.

Hence it seems possible to conclude, taking the above views into consideration, that the *Ragulae* has its own influence on the later writings of Descartes. If this is the case, then let us see in more detail how Descartes carried on his programme to frame his epistemology in the *Meditations* and in the *Principles of Philosophy* taking the *rules* into consideration.

The *Discours de la Mathode*, which is supposed to give the idea of methodology of Descartes to carry out his further programme, does not give sufficient account of his method. In other words, a fuller account of the *Discours* can only be given provided the *Regulae* is to be taken into consideration. While giving his account of epistemology, I would discuss that in connection with earlier and later versions and would try to suggest how are they connected.

Let us begin with the earlier assumptions of his epistemology, which starts from the *Regulae*. In the *Regulae*, Descartes deals with the following problems :

1. To define in exact and rigorous terms what we should mean by *knowledge*
2. To determine the method to be followed in its pursuit, and
3. To determine whether there are limits beyond which we cannot hope to advance, and if such limits are there, to define them exactly.

These are the implications of his third and fourth rules mentioned in the *Regulae*. In them he gave a preliminary account of *intuition* and *deduction* and claimed that only through these two, can indubitable knowledge be achieved ?

In the *Regulae*, Descartes did not talk of the doctrine of *innate ideas* and of *representative perception*. Rather he adopted an empirical realist's view which holds that objects are directly apprehended by the mind. That apprehension takes place in an immediate face-to-face manner and at the same time he also accepted the possibility of knowledge of external objects.

But subsequently, Descartes became aware of the incompleteness of the account of the sources of knowledge in the *Regulae*. That made him to accept an *aliquid amplius* and to account for that, he adopted a doctrine of *innate*-ideas,[10] which I would discuss later on.

As another epistemological assumption for right understanding, Descartes adopted the phrase *clear* and *distinct*, which consistently occurs throughout his writings.[11] And in application of this clear and distinct perception, he wants to explain the immediate experience of face-to-face manner so that the apprehension would be clear *even to rustics.* This capacity for immediate face-to-face awareness cannot be fallacious, for this reason he elsewhere speaks of the *natural light of reason,* which I would mention later on.

The problem of the meaning of "*clear and distinct perception*" is really the central issue in the interpretation of the method, which played a vital role at the heart of Descartes' philosophy. If the *Principles of Philosophy* is taken into account, we find "In our early years our mind is so immersed in the body that it knows nothing *distinctly,* though it apprehends much sufficiently *clearly* . . . forming many judgments and and contracting many prejudices from which the majority of us can hardly ever hope to become free". He continued further, "I term that *clear* which is present and manifest to an attentive mind just as we are said to see objects clearly when, being present to the intuiting eye, they operate upon it sufficiently strongly and manifestly. But the *distinct* is that which is so precise and different from all other objects that it contains within itself only what appears manifestly to him who considers it as he ought . . . when, for instance, an intense pain is felt, our awareness of it is very clear, but is not always distinct; for men usually confound it with their obscure judgements as to its nature, assuming as they do, that in the part affected their exists something similar to the sensation of pain of which alone they are clearly aware. *Thus a cognition can be clear without being distinct; but can never be distinct without being also clear*"[12]

This distinction as well as the analysis regarding clear and distinct perception of the *Discours* is in agreement with that of the *Regulae*; therefore, N. K. Smith has rightly remarked that the attitude of Descartes regarding clear and distinct perception continued to be same throughout his later writings, without change. Even Boyce Gibson remarked that the clear and distinct perceptions dealt in the *Discours* are more elaborately dealt in the *Regulae*; "The most complete exposition of the clear and distinct ideas is to be found in the *Regulae de inquirenda veritate,* though popular resume is included in the theory of *Discours.* In both works the dominating theme is the quest for certaintly and universal knowledge."[13]

To substantiate the above point furthert Rule IX of the

Regulae should be taken into consideration, which states, "we ought to give the whole of our attention to the most insignificant and most easily mastered facts, and remain a long time in contemplation of them until we are accustomed to behold the truth *clearly* and *distinctly*."[14] Even the phrase clearly and distinctly, occurs once in the *Regulae*, sufficiently justify the relationship with later matured works of Descartes.

In the *Regulae*, two important ways of acquiring knowledge are, *intuition* and *deduction*. The intuition, which Descartes admitted in the *Regulae* would be equivalent to the clear and distinct perception of the *Meditations*.[15] While explaining this, Descartes accepted in the *Regulae* that the two things are required for mental intuition. One is that the proposition intuited must be clear and distinct and secondly, it must be grasped in its totality at the same time and not successively. This presupposes the concrete epistemology which Descartes advocated in his later writings. Descartes admitted that the "intuition, not the fluctuating testimony of the senses, nor the misleading judgement that proceeds from the blundering constructions of imagination, but the conception which an unclouded and attentive mind gives us so readily and distinctly that we are wholly freed from doubt about that which we understand."[16] In addition to intuition, Descartes' another method of knowing, that is knowing by *deduction*. But he explained that the deduction is subject to memory, while *intuition* is free from all limitations. Rather the intuition assumed here is natural light of reason or *Lumen naturale*, which was in general use in 17th century. Descartes further asserted that this *Lumen Naturale* helps in clear and distinct understanding.

As it has already been mentioned, *clear and distinct* perception is equivalent to 'intuition' of the *Regulae*, it provides sufficient reason, why Descartes dropped the use of the term 'intuition' for 'clear' and 'distinct' in his later writings. Because in the *Ragulae* it is explicitly stated that for acquisition of knowledge 'intuition' is the primary factor, which aims at clear and distinct perception and that has been simply revived as the function of 'clear' and 'distinct' in the *Meditations*.

The study of the *Regulae* revealed further that besides intuition and *deduction*, Descartes also spoke of *Divine Certainty* which he stated concretely in the *Meditations* in the form of Veracity of God. To quote the *Regulae* in tbis connection, "These two methods are the most certain routes to knowledge, and the mind should admit no others. All the rest should be rejected as suspect of error and dangerous. But this does not prevent us from believing matters that have been Divinely revealed as being more certain than our surest knowledge, since belief in these things as all faith in obscure matters, is an action not of our intelligence (ingenii) but of our will."[17]

While giving an account of acquisition of knowledge, the term *experience* and its use in the *Regulae* should be taken into consideration, because it presupposes the concrete epistemology, which Descartes demonstrates in later writings. Descartes' use of the term experience in the *Regulue,* helps in understanding the terms *intuition* and *deduction.* Therefore, experience' as used in the *Ragulae* should be understood in its immediate non-fallacious aspect. Here Descartes seems to be very careful, because, he never intended to equate immediate experience with sense experience. He used 'experience' in two aspects, first is the commonsense every-day awareness of the external world, which he claims sharply as frequently fallacious,[18] but the other is the immediate awareness in the sense of *Lumen Naturale*, which aims at clear and distinct perception. Thereafter it is clear, Descartes' use of 'experience' in the *Regulae* always indicates its immediate non-fallacious aspect which aims at achievement of indubitable knowledge. This analysis of 'experience' suggests as if Descartes had laid the foundation stone of his later epistemology in the *Ragulae* itself. Because the rationalistic assumptions were clear while he claimed that 'experience' is more often fallacious. He even claimed that the scientific understanding in the form of *clear* and *distinct* can never be achieved by sensible experience, because the sensory experience only attends to the 'appearences'. For this reason his deductive method, he denied to be syllogistic in nature, rather he made it very clear that the deduction is nothing but series of intuitions. The *intuition*, which Descartes accepted in the *Regulae* is free from any type of mystic interpretation rather it is taken as the foundation of all scientific knowledge, whose other title would be *Lumen Naturale.*

Whether this *Lumen Naturale.* would be another title of

intuition or not, has become a controversial issue in the writings of Descartes. Because commentators like John Morris[19] upheld the opinion that both these "Natural Fight of Reason" and "Intuition" cannot be substituted. However the fact remains that Descartes did not clarify the role of the *Natural Light* and its relationship to *reason* explicitly, which he has done in the *Meditations*, but taking John Morris' view into consideration one can conclude that Descartes was using these concepts in traditional sense.

One more epistemological assumption Descartes raised in the *Discours* and *Meditations*, is that of *Hyperbolical doubt* in order to arrive at contain knowledge, which has become an important part of Descartes' methodology since the beginning. As a result of this programme Descartes speaks of '*cogito ergo sum*' as our sole indubitable certainty in the *Discours*. In this connection if the *Regulae* is to be studied, the method of doubt does not appear there in hyperbolical form, because at that time Descartes completely abstained from all deep metaphysical speculations. He was rather deeply concerned with methodological aspects of his programme. But in the *Regulae* the doubt occurs in some places devoid of its hyperbolical element. At this point one can very well visualize the farsight of Descartes, how he dealt only with rules pertaining to methodology in his early unfinished treatise, keeping the corresponding metaphysical issues for the later works.

The method of doubt employed in the *Regulae* was not at all sceptical, rather it aims at a selection of clear and distinct truths known intuitively. To deal this point in more detail, we find no trace of hyperbolical doubt in the *Regulae* because of two reasons.

1. By that time Descartes was pre-occupied with Arithematical and Geometrical assumptions. He was of opinion that these disciplines are free from any taint of falsity, bacause they are exclusively based on intuition.

2. In the *Regulae* there is no suggestion that immagination is opposed to understanding and the immediate face-to-face awareness is different from judgment. That is why, Descartes did not question by what right we can claim to pass judgments on what is not accessible to direct awareness, such as, the nature of existence of God etc. It is only in subsequent years, that he

could realise that immediate awareness and judgment, immediate awareness and experience should be treated separately. In consequence of the above assumptions, in order to account for the existence of God and for the distinctive characteristics of mathematical disciplines, he had to adopt the doctrine of innate-ideas in his later writings for his concrete epistemology.

His use of the term ***experience*** in face-to-face manner which calls upon *Lumen Naturale* and his explanation of this intuition in the line of clear and distinct perception in the *Regulae*, amply suggests an epistemology which became explicit in the later writings.

The concrete epistemology which appeared in later works of Descartes centers around the doctrine of innate-ideas. My central concern would be to see how the *Regulae* anticipated the metaphysical speculations of later works and how the methodological aspect of the programme has been dealt with carefully to achieve certainty in the matters of knowledge.

To begin with, in the later works Descartes gave due *attention to ideas, not as objects of direct awareness but in their representative capacity*, which provides us knowledge of what is additional to them. While separating judgments from immediate awareness he claims that in judgment there is presence of *aliquid-amplius* and this *aliquide-amplius* not only calls a doctrine of innate-ideas but also for a doctrine of natural belief. This is the programme of Descartes, to arrive at a revolutionary theory of knowledge corresponding to the current metaphysical trend.

In a passage in the *Meditations*[20] Descartes clearly stated how an *aliquid-amplius* distinguishes judgment from immediate awareness. There, Descartes claimed that what is known sensuously through pineal patterns is imagination which are fluctuating and what is known rationally through common notions and axioms is understanding, which is constant and universal. The images are apprehended through immediate face-to-face awareness but the common notions and exioms are innate notions, by the help of which we can obtain scientific understanding even of *appearances*.

In order to give an account of sensuous and rational knowledge, Descartes divided the ideas in *Meditation III*, as below:

"I find present to me completely diverse ideas of the sun; the one, in which the sun appears to me as extremely small, is, it would seem, derived from the senses, and to be counted as belonging to the class of adventitious ideas, the other, in which the sun is taken to be many times larger than the whole Earth, has been arrived at by way of astronomical reasoning, that is to say, elicited from certain notions innate in me, or formed by me in some other manner."[21]

This above classification of ideas into adventitious and innate in the *III Meditations* has been accepted as provisional. But elsewhere in a letter to Mersenne, Descartes has improved upon it. Descartes wrote in 1641:

"Some ideas are adventitious, such as the idea we commonly have of the sun, other are factitious, in which class we can put the idea which the astronomers construct of the sun by their reasoning, and others are innate, such as the idea of God, Mind, Body, triangle and in general all those which represent true immutable, and eternal essences."[22]

Subsequently, we find some controversy as to the division of ideas in Descartes himself. However this tripartite classification of ideas given in the *III Meditations*, have been superseded lateron only to innate ideas forming a class of themselves.

In this connection, if the *Regulae* is also studied, it seems that Descartes also assumed a classification of ideas, while he was dealing with Rule XII. He said: "It is properly called mind when it either forms new ideas in the fancy, or attends to those already formed."[23] Leaving this classification, if his notion of simples of the *Regulae* is to be considered, we see how Descartes reduced everything to 'simple notions' because they are wholly free from falsity. The examples of 'simple notions' of the *Regulae* such as, figure, extension, motion, etc., clearly resembles the innate ideas of the *Meditations*. Even in the *Regulae*. Descartes further asserted that those 'simple notions' are purely intellectual which our understanding apprehends by means of a certain inborn light, and without the aid of any corporeal image.[24]

In the *Regulae* we also find Descartes was beginning to be

conscious of the distinction between immediate awareness and judgments. From his letter to Mersenne (1630), Descartes holds that 'will' and 'understanding' operate very differently in God and in Man. God's actions are creative, but in Man, the understanding is passively receptive and is finite. One definite and consistent point that Descartes makes is that in cognitive awareness the understanding is *patiently receptive.* It is never creative of its ideas, rather it combines or separates them, which has been disclosed to us by *Lumen Naturale.* In order to account for these ideas in the *Regulae*, Descartes talks of ideas in *pure intellectuals Vel pure materiales* and *Vel communes.* But subsequently his metaphysical speculations gave the idea of incomplete division, because the classification never includes sensations and passions, which depend upon the union of the mind and the body hence cannot be assigned to either purely to mind or purely to body.

The existence of God, which Descartes advocated in his later writings in order to certify the certainty of clear and distinct perception has become a controversial issue. Apart from this the fact remains that knowledge of God cannot be apprehended through direct awareness; no inference and analogy can give us the knowledge of God. To account for the knowledge of God, Descartes adopted that, it is only through an innate-idea that God can be known. Gradually, he claimed existence of innumerable innate-ideas, forming a class and the doctrine of *cogito-ergosum* is an example of this class.

If the comparison would be made between judgments of mathematics and *cogito* judgments, we find Descartes, in the line of Plato. As Plato claimed in the *Meno,* that geometrical assumptions are innately there in the human mind, Descartes argued that as we have never in our lives seen a true triangle, or an accurately drawn circle, we could not derive these ideas from sensation. When we see physical triangle, we are simply reminded of the true and immutable nature of the triangle; we recognize it when we see that. This ability to recognize an instance of a concept is probably what Descartes means by an innate-idea. To quote Descartes, "so, indeed, we should not be able to recognize the geometrical triangle by looking at that which is drawn on paper, unless our mind possessed an idea of it derived from some other source."[25]

This, 'some other source' clearly indicates the existence of innate faculties in the mind, which is more certain than mathematical and geometrical assumptions. Therefore *cogito* judgments of the *Meditations* clearly aims at innate possession of human mind which is more certain than mathematical assumptions. If we substantiate this point further we see that Descartes is not committing any inconsistency.

In the *Regulae*, mathematical and geometrical assumptions have been accepted as certain, where as in the *Meditations* they are subjects to doubt. Apparently one may find an inconsistency here but actually Descartes is consistent so far as doubting is concerned; because in both the works (The *Regulae* and the *Meditations*) Descartes is dealing with methodical doubt,[26] not with *experimental doubt*. The experimental doubt, refers to a certain state of mind or attitude which does not voluntarily originate, while the methodical doubt refers, not to a feeling, but to a decision or volition which we do purposively originate. Further, the methodical doubt is different from scepticism, while experimental doubt frequently contributes to 'sceptical frame of mind'. If this analysis is taken into consideration, we don't find any inconsistency so far as the *Regulae* and the *Meditations* are concerned. Both refer to methodical doubt, none inspires experimental doubt.

(ii) Innate Ideas and the Cartesian Philosophy of Mind

So far I have dealt with the earlier and later works of Descartes and their relationship to one another to find out the crucial role played by the doctrine of innate-ideas in his epistemology. This doctrine which has become central in epistemology induces a discussion of his *philosophy of mind*, otherwise the doctrine would collapse. Because the doctrine of innate-ideas and the nature of mind, depend upon each other for their explanation, one would lose its meaning in isolation of the other.

Descartes' methodology leading to his epistemology clearly suggests a philosophy of mind, which he has developed consistently with his own speculations. His doctrine of innate-ideas, which I have discussed taking his own methodological programme, would become incomplete unless his psychology is also taken into consideration. Therefore, in this section, I shall concentrate on his explanation of the status of sensation with regard to his conception of soul or how his conception of mind is distinct or different from sensation. Subsequently, it would be seen how his mind-body dualism emerges out of the doctrine of innate-ideas.

While explaining the conception of mind or sonl in Descartes, I shall take the following aspects into consideration—*intuition*, *power of reason* and *will*.

Intuition is the primary example of grasping a truth. By means of intuition alone we know the innate capacities of the mind. The innate ideas in the mind would mean that our knowledge is determined in accordance with certain principles and concepts which are native endowment of all minds. Those cannot be acquired by abstraction from sense-experience. While explaining this Descartes argued that concepts corresponding to the simple natures, such as, geometrical points, line, circle, equality etc., cannot be derived or acquired but they are *primitive* and *innate* in thinking. In this sense of 'innate', all ideas that are ideas of simple natures are innate. These innate-ideas can be apprehended only by an operation, known as *intuition* (intuitus) which is innate in the sense of not acquired. All clear and distinct ideas derivable from them are innate because they can be produced only through an operation known as deduction (*deductio*), which is also innate. Because this intuition and deduction are, "mental operations by which we are able, entirely without any fear of illusion to arrive at the knowledge of things."[27] Intuition is purely an intellectual activity, which in return is *clear* and distinct, because it leaves no room for doubt. By means of this intuition, one attends to the *simple natures* which are *innate*. The outstanding characteristic of those *simple natures*, as accepted by Descartes, are their perfect clearness and distinctness. But with only intuition, the human knowledge would seem to be incomplete, because it only gives knowledge of first principles. From these first principles, again the mind by means of its *power of reason* deduces further knowledge. To quote Descartes, "But the first principles themselves are given by intuition alone, while on the countrary the remote conclusions are furnised only by deduction."[28] While explaining the nature of deduction Descartes affirms that in the steps of deductive procedure intuition plays a dominant role, because for him deduction is but a series of intuitions.

Finally, everything depends upon the *free will* which is a freedom of the human mind. We use this freedom rightly when we affirm only what is quite clear and distinct and refarin from assenting what is not clear. Because we are not compelled to determine in the use of our will, we may suspend judgment, otherwise we can give an assent. This freedom we exercise in yielding or withholding assent is the single characteristic which we possess, which resembles the nature of God. If so, then how does error arise? Here Descartes' explanation would be that the will be dominated by inclinations of body but as God is bodiless animal there this question never arises. But in case of man, when the bodily inclinations predominate, it loses its will by surrendering to passions. But when the will attends to the clear and distinct principles, the human mind achieves perfection similar to the nature of God.

These above aspects of the mind constitute the essential nature of the soul. They do not have anything in common with the body, which presupposes his fundamental problem of mind and body.[29]

This would be more clear, if due consideration is given to the *passions of the soul* (*Les Passions de L'Ame*), the earliest physiological theory of the emotions, advocated by Descartes. That work has been regarded as *'over-intellectualized'*.[30] In that work, Descartes elaborately dealt with the passions and claimed that passions are not actions of the soul; rather they are emotions of the soul caused by the body. The passions depend on and are excited by psychological conditions. They are caused by the movements of the animal spirit. But on the other hand, the clear and distinct perceptions are actions of the soul only. They do not have anything to do with passions, which are caused by bodily motions. Therefore it is clear, how the epistemological dualism of knowledge and experience is a consequence of the ontological dualism of materiality and mentality. Because knowing being a function of the souls intrinsic nature, it is logically independent of the knowers body and its activities. This line of thought in Descartes initiates a discussion on the *role of sense-experience in the construction of knowledge.* To Descartes, sense-experience has no direct epistemological value, it is only instrumental in supplying the occasion on which the intellect becomes actively engaged. In other words, sense experience furnishes the occasion on which the mind recognizes innate-ideas and by experience only we become aware that there are external objects corresponding to our ideas. Though the self-experience is sometimes instrumentally useful in acquisition of knowledge, in Descartes' opinion, it is never constitutive of that knowledge. Because they more often conceal than reveal the genuine character of things. However, the fact remains that the epistemological analysis given by Descartes seems to be the rudimentaly form of Kantian epistemology, which we find a century and a half later. Nevertheless one can claim that the epistemology of Descartes in the above lines is likely to be more convincing than that of Locke, who claims the mind to be a *tabula rasa* and experience as the only source of knowledge.

Having explained the nature and operation of mind, we now have to see that *Intuition*, *Power of Reason* and *will*, do not have anything to do with the body. The *intuition*, which is supposed to be the primary criterion of grasping truth, has nothing to do with bodily actions. But by the help of the intuition, we prehend in separation non-sensible natures and ideas. Intuition is the direct act of prehension by means of which clear and distinct perception takes place. This clear and distinct perception, which is the criterion of truth has nothing to do with the bodily movements. In order to explain this point further, we may consider it from two angles.

Firstly, our minds cannot be caused to think the primal ideas, which Descartes thought to be innate, by the actions of material bodies, such causal actions would be nothing other than movements. If a particular movement would cause the mind to think clearly and distinctly about anything at all, it could cause it to think about itself, because the movement being particular the thought would be of a particular. But axioms and common notions are neither of particulars nor of movements. Hence, material bodies and their changes could not be the cause of our thinking axioms and common notions.

Secondly, to suppose that a particular movement could cause the mind to think of it, is also not admissible, because modes of matter can cause nothing but other modes of matter.

Material bodies and their actions cannot cause thoughts of clear and distinct ideas to occur, because physical actions and thoughts are modes of two mutually exclusive attributes. An event or state (mode) of one order cannot cause an event or state in another order. Therefore, no clear and distinct thought is reached from sensible appearances, nor they are caused by changes in material bodies. Rather those clear and distinct thoughts, which are supposed to be innate, are only approachable to intuition, which is also an innate faculty of the human mind.

The power of deducing, which is supposed to be the *power of reason,* has nothing to do with bodily changes, for, Descartes accepted deduction in a very special sense. For him deduction is nothing but a series of; intuitions in other words, it is an *extended intuition.* Similarly, the *freedom of will,* Descartes took, to be an innate-notion. Therefore, he states that "finally it is so evident that we are possessed of a free-will that can give or withhold its assent, that this may be counted as one of the first and most ordinary notions that are found innately in us".[31]

Hence, it is seen that *intuition, power of reason* and *will,* have nothing to do with the material body. They are supposed to be *innate capacities* of the mind. Those capacities only contribute towards the construction of knowledge, while the bodily actions are instrumental to that. The pertinent point comes out here, that the doctrine of innate idea brings a dualism, in order to demonstrate a rational explanation of Descartes epistemology.

To substantiate further the concept of innate-idea, we find, it is not merely a hypothesis or a doctrine, but a philosophical principle occupying a central place in Descartes epistemology. His doctrine of innate ideas does not merely contribute to his epistemology, but has its own bearing even in physics.[32] This line of argument amply suggests how Descartes has presented an integrated system. Starting from his earliest work the *Regulae* to the latest works like the *Passions of the Soul* and the *Letters* are so connected to each other. It seems as if they construct a "whole" where all of his other works become parts. He has presented such a neatly woven system, that no part of his philosophy can be studied in isolation from the other. The Rules leading to the direction of Mind, Methodology, Metaphysics, Physics, epistemology and Moral philosophy, all are so linked with each other that acceptance of one, involves the acceptance of others. Therefore, once he has rightly remarked that:

> "Thus philosophy as a whole is like a tree whose roots are metaphysics, whose trunk is physics, and whose branches, which issue from this trunk, are all the other sciences."[33]

Leaving apart the Metaphorical elements from the above statement, it shows the underlying profoundity of his philosophy as a whole and how they merge together to form a unity. For example, taking any philosophical concept from any part of his work, if one wants to move around, ultimately he would find himself in the same place, from where he had started. But his critics like Locke, committed blunders by considering his philosophy in part. However, we find some deficiencies here and there relating to innate ideas,[34] but in my view philosophical deficiencies are not at all a deficiency, rather they constitute fundamental problems to the future generation.

Descartes, being the founder of modern philosophy, started a systematic endeavour to clear out this long-felt philosophical prejudices up to the Renaissance and has shown how philosophizing can be dealt with very methodically. As a consequence of this, besides other works, he has started a philosophy of mind and he was certainly the first to have worked out the directive ideas of a psychology in our modern sense of the word.[35]

Leaving aside his multifarious philosophical achievements. he left many formidable philosophical issues to the future generation. Examples would be, his doctrine of innate-ideas in so far preparatory of Kant's *Categories of Understanding*, his *a priori* concepts and principles lead to the *synthetic a priori judgments of Kant* and more particularly the current thought, *Philosophy of Language*, which has become sensational from Noam Chomsky's *Cartesian Linguistics*.[36]

REFERENCES

1. Cp., Adam and Tannery, X, pp. 530-2 and XII pp. 146ff.

1. Cf., H. Joachim, *Descartes' Rules for the Direction of the Mind,* (George Allen and Unwin, London: 1957) p. 13.
2. Cf., H. Joachim, p. 13.
3. Cf., Haldane and Rose., *Philosophical Works of Descartes.,* (from Prefatory Note), Dover Publications, Inc., 1955.
4. Op. cit., H. Joachim., p. 14.
5. Op. cit., Haldane and Ross., Vol. I, (from Prefatory Note).
6. "The Basis of Knowledge in Descartes", originally published in MIND, Vol. XXXVIII, No. 151, July 1929, pp. 330-342, and No. 152, October 1929, pp. 458-472. Again reprinted with minor revisions in Modern Studies in Philosophy Series, *Descartes,* ed., Doney, pp. 169-191. (Macmillan, 1968).
7. Leon Roth., *Descartes' Discours on Method,* (Oxford: 1937) pp. 63-64.
8. Ibid., p. 64-65.
9. S. V. Keeling., *Descartes,* (Oxford: 1968) Cf. 62 ff.
10. Cf., N. K. Smith, *New Studies in the Philosophy of Descartes,* (Macmillan, London: 1963) p. 53.
11. Once in the *Regulae,* but in the Meditations over 30 times (Cf. N. K. Smith, *New Studies in the Philosophy of Descartes,* p. 55).
12. Haldane and Ross., Vol. I, p. 237 (Cf. *New Studies in the Philosophy of Descartes.,* N. K. Smith, pp. 59-60).
13. Boyce Gibson, *The Philosophy of Descartes,* (Mathuen & Co., London: 1932) pp. 151-152.
14. Op. cit., Haldane and Ross, *Reg.* IX, Vol. I, p. 28.
15. Op. cit., Doney, ed. *Descartes,* p. 188.
16. Op. cit., Haldane and Ross., Vol. I, p. 7.
17. Ibid., p. 8.
18. Ibid., p. 4.
19. "Descartes Natural Light", *Journal of History of Philosophy,* April 1973, Vol. XI, No. 2., May be seen for further information.
20. *Meditations* III; (Descartes Philosophical Works, (D. P. W.) Trans. N. K. Smith, 1952) pp. 215-216. (Cf. *New Studies in the Philosophy of Descartes,* N. K. Smith, Macmillan, London: 1963. p. 233).
    In this passage Descartes also takes account of desire and volition. In their case the *aliquid amplius* is the 'desired' and the 'willed' as distinguished from the 'judged', i.e. from the affirmed or denied.
21. *Med. III; D. P. W.,* p. 218 (Cf. Op. cit, N. K. Smith, *New Studies in the Philosophy of Descartes,* p. 236).
22. Charles Adam and Paul Tannery (A. T.) *Med.* III (Cf. Op. cit., N. K. Smith, *New Studies in the Philosophy of Descartes,* p. 236.
23. Op. cit., Haldane and Ross, Vol. I, p. 39.
24. Ibid., Vol. I, p. 41.
25. Ibid., Vol. II, pp. 227-228.
26. Cf. Op. cit., S. V. Keeling, pp. 87-88.
27. Regulae—3, A. T. x, 368, H. & R. III p. 7.
28. Regulae—3, A. T. x, 370, H. & R. III p. 8.

29. In order to explain his representative theory of perception, Descartes sometimes admit a ***substantial union*** between mind and body, which resulted in theory of occasionalism. But to say that mind occasionally attends to body, is to say that it is a mystery.
30. One exception to these objectors is Prof. D. Irons. He adds: "Though written in the earliest days of modern science, this work (the Passions) will bear comparison with anything that has been produced in recent years. It will be difficult indeed to find any treatment of the emotions much superior to it in originality, Thoroughness and suggestiveness" (*Philosophical Review*, 1895, p. 291) (Cf. Op. cit., *Descartes*, S. V. Keeling., p. 290).
31. Op. cit., Haldane and Ross, Vol. I, p. 234.
32. Cf. Op. cit., F. Copleston, *A History of Philosophy*, Vol. IV., p. 84.
33. Op. cit., Haldane and Ross, Vol. I, p. 211.
34. Op. cit., S. V. Keeiing, *Descartes*: "Unfortunately his (Descartes) theory of innateness is not worked out so fully and clearly as we could wish". (p. 182) "Descartes, it cannot be denied, fails to work-out fully or clearly enough, his theory of innate-ideas" (p. 293) Out of these two remarks it seems Descartes' explanation for innate-ideas is not sufficiently dealt with.
35. Cf., Ibid., p. 291.
36. Noam Chomsky, *Cartesian Linguistics*, (N. Y., Harper and Row, 1966).

5

Locke's Critique of Innate Ideas: An Assessment

INTRODUCTION

Descartes' philosophy in general and the doctrine of innate ideas in particular would be clear only after the discussion of John Locke, who is supposed to be the greatest critic of Descartes, an assumption which needs of course a further clarification. John Locke's famous work *An Essay Concerning Human Understanding* (1690) would be my sole study, while discussing his philosophy my important concern would be as follows; taking Locke's criticism of innate ideas[1] into consideration, I would discuss, how the polemic has become controversial, (here I would throw light on positive and negative aspects of the polemic). I would reveal the contention then, that Locke's recognition of non-sensory sources of knowledge and its analysis never supports his polemic and subsequently how Locke failed to supply a corresponding philosophy of mind to his conception of knowledge. And I would conclude the discussion, showing how Locke's theory of knowledge involved an account of rationalism; here my main concern would be to see, whether Locke is an empiricist or a rationalist.

The first Book of the *Essay* where Locke deals with the

polemic begins with, "It is an established opinion amongst some men, that there are in the understanding certain *innate principles*; some primary notions, characters, as it were stamped upon the mind of man; which the soul receives in its very first being, and brings into the world with it."[2] This passage of Locke in the very beginning of the chapter became controversial, because he did not mention particularly to whom the polemic was directed. However, the fact remains that Locke's polemic raised a very concerted effort towards the epistemology as a whole and doctrine of innate-ideas in particular.

Locke's polemic, besides its element of controversy, needs a further clarification in order to justify its significance taking the then prevailing situation into consideration. The traditional answer as to against whom the polemic directed was Descartes. But when scholars came to realise Locke's own debt to Descartes and re-discovered the rational element in his writings and when they examined Descartes' doctrine of innate-ideas more critically, they concluded that this answer was not satisfactory. Then, if Descartes and the Cartesians were not Locke's target, the obvious question was to search after his real opponents.[3]

However apart from the controversy the modified version of the traditional answer given by Aaron[4] may be taken into consideration. According to him, in the first place, the attack is aimed at Descartes and the Cartesians. But it is also aimed with equal force at various English thinkers and teachers, moralists and theologians of his own day. Taking support of both Leibniz[5] and Voltaire[6] Aaron was driven to the conclusion that, "Both of them assumed without question that in Book I Locke was attacking Descartes and the Cartesians."[7] Provisionally taking Descartes as the target of Locke's polemic, let us see further its consequences.

(i) Locke's Criticism of Innate-Ideas

In order to establish the empiricist foundations of knowledge, Locke first started arguments against the theory of innate principles. Locke understands this theory as being the doctrine that "there are in the understanding certain innate principles; some primary notions, characters, as it were stamped upon the mind of man; which the soul receives in the very first being, and brings into the world with it."[8] Some of these principles are speculative; whose examples would be 'whatever is, is, and it is impossible for the something to be and not to be.' Others are practical, such as general moral principles.

The important argument according to Locke is the one regarding the *Universal Consent*. Because all men agree about the Validity of certain speculative and practical principles those principles are originally imprinted on men's minds and that they brought them into the world with them "as necessary and really as they do any of their inherent faculties."[9]

Against the above theory Locke argues that even if it were true that all men agree about certain principles this would not prove that these principles are innate, provided that some other explanation can be given of this universal consent.

Secondly, Locke opines that the arguments which were brought in favour of the theory of innate principles, were worthiless, because there is no universal consent about the truth of any principle. Children and idiots have minds, but they have no knowledge of the principle that it is impossible for something to be and not to be. He continued further and asserted that if these principles were really innate, then they must be known. Therefore, he categorically remarked that "No proposition can be said to be in the mind, which it never yet knew, which it was never yet conscious of."[10] In other words, ideas cannot be held mentally in a latent or unconcious state, there cannot be impressions made on the mind without accompanying consciousness of them, because of a mental impression and a consciousness of it are identical. No ideas can said to be *in the mind* of which that mind is not either actually percipient, or through memory capable of becoming percipient. To illustrate this, Locke states that, "a great part of illiterate people and savages pass many years, even of their rational age, without ever thinking on this and the like general propositions."[11] He took the same position towards practical and moral principles.[12]

The defender of innate principles may argue that all these possibilities would be true only, when people came to use reason. To this Locke's answer would be, that there are men who apprehend no general abstract principles at all. Locke did not deny that there are principles of this kind, but he refused to admit that there is any sufficient reason for calling them innate.

The defenders of innate principles talk about a knowledge which is ohly *implicit*, by which they mean a *capacity for knowledge*. That *capacity* itself is innate. In return Locke assumes throughout that the mind has *inherent faculties*, which it brings into the world with it.[13] Further to remove the confusion, amongst the defenders, Locke wrote on a margin of Burnet's 'Remarks on the Essay' that, "I think nobody who reads my book can doubt that I spoke only of *innate-ideas* and not *innate-powers*."[14] Even with regards to the mathematical propositions, he does not prefer to call innate-propositions, rather he considered that out of such a misuse of language only confusion anc misunderstanding could result. In order to justify his stand, he categorically mentioned that innate-principles are not "a distinct sort of truth" which is regarded by Locke as equivalent to the abandonment of the theory.[15]

So far as the above arguments are concerned, one would find it very difficult to assume that Descartes is the target of the polemic. Throughout the polemic it seems Locke was attacking only *innate principles*, but not to the *doctrine of innate ideas*. But considering the true spirit inherent in the threads of the argument one would be driven to a dilemma of *innate-principles* and *innate ideas*. However it seems very clear as we have seen that Descartes also did not clearly draw a distinction between *ideas* and *principles*, which would be in return help to infer that Locke was not attacking Descartes. Similarly, Locke also very often spoke of innate-notions, which is equivalent to innate-ideas. Secondly, Locke's contrast between *innate* and *adventitious* ideas seems to be directly drawn from the Cartesian distinction.

The *positive* element of the polemic certainly brings out a clear understanding of the role of experience, which was not explicit in Descartes' epistemology. In other words the incomplete explanation of Descartes is being supplied by Locke which gives enough consideration to the role of experience. While in Descartes experience is needed as the occasion on which the mind brings forth from itself materials, which it previously contained only virtually but they can be in no sense produced by experience, but in Locke that very experience constitutes the essence of knowledge. The fundamental and philosophical distinction between both was only concerning the questions of method rather than of substance. Because Descartes assumed the very existence of experience without going deep into that while Locke questioned the very fundamental role of experience. Of course one should not blame one by accepting the views of the other. Because both differ in their attitude regarding their approach to epistemology as a whole. While Descartes was above all a system builder to whose temper the critical attitude of Locke was entirely foreign. Descartes was insisting that the foundation of well grounded certainty is only to be reached by the attempt to render doubt universal and having obtained his indubitable starting point, he was discovering the true method by means of which a connected system of knowledge might emerge to lead us towards certainty, where the role of experience was justifiably insignificant. On the other hand, in case of Locke, he was not attempting to furnish any new method of knowledge, rather his aim was "not to teach men a new way of certainty . . . . but to endeavour to show wherein the old and only way of certainty consists."[16] He asserted further regarding his role that "it is ambition enough to be employed as an underlabour in clearing the ground a little and removing some of the rubbish that lies in the way of knowledge."[17] Instead of seeking a method which enable us to proceed dogmatically, he proclaims the need of criticism. Therefore as a true believer of his own spirit, instead of accepting experience, he questioned the very fundamental role of experience, which in return becomes a virtue of his own epistemology. Therefore one should not claim that the empiricism of Locke is an alternative to rationalism of Descartes, rather it supplied material to make rationalism more effective.

The *negative* element of the polemic constitutes Locke's recognition of non-sensory sources of knowledge. Such as—*intuition* and *demonstration*. His acceptance of three degrees of knowledge in *Book IV of the Essay* deserves a consideration here.

Intuition: For Locke knowledge is "the perception of the connection of and agreement, or disagreement and repugnancy if any of our ideas."[18] He claimed further that sometimes the mind perceives the agreement or disagreement of two ideas immediately, wirhout intervention of anyother; that is called *intuition knowledge.*[19] For example, that white is not black, that a circle is not a triangle, that three are more than two and equal to one and two. This kind of knowledge is "the clearest and most certain that human fraility is capable of. This part of knowledge is irresistible, and, like bright sunshine, forces itself immediately to be perceived, as soon as ever the mind turns its view that way."[20]

The next degree of knowledge is where the mind proceeds to discover the agreement or disagreement of ideas by the intervention of other ideas, called *demonstrative knowledge.* Each step of *demonstration* must have *intuitive evidence* or in other words demonstration is nothing but a series of intuitions. These two kinds, intuitive and demonstrative, are the only kinds of knowledge properly so-called. The third degree of knowledge, *Sensitive knowledge,* "passes under the name of the knowledge,"[21] but whose account is not very detailed or careful.

Locke's acceptance of *intuition* as the ground of certainty very much resembles to *intuitionism* of Descartes and needs a further clarification.

The intuitionism of Descartes was most explicitly dealt in his *Regulae* where he distinguishes *intuitus,* which is the term he uses for *intellectual intuition* sharply from *sensory intuition* and from imagination. In the third rule of the *Regulae,*[22] he explains how *intuitus* is "not the fluctuating testimony of the senses, nor the misleading judgment that proceeds from the blundering constructions of imagination, but the pure intellectual orgnizing of which an unclouded and attentive mind is capable; a cognizing so ready and so distinct that we are wholly freed from doubt about that which we thus intellectually apprehend." To sum up, in intuitive knowing the mind is fully aware, unclouded wholly attentive and entirely free from doubt. In the *Regulae* and even in the *Principia,* Descartes emphasized mind's full activity in *intuitive knowledge.* Using this intuitionism as a spectacle of Descartes, one can look at Locke's celebrated Essay, particularly Book IV, as to find out the similarities.[23]

Locke in Book IV of the *Essay* in a similar fashion speaks: "Certainty depends so wholly on this intuition, that, in the next degree of knowledge which I call demonstrative, this intuition is necessary in all the connections of the intermediate ideas, without which we cannot attain knowledge and certainty."[24]. Further asserted: "Now, in every step reason makes in demonstrative knowledge, there is an intuitive knowledge of that agreement or disagreement it seeks with the next intermediate idea which it use as proof. . . . By which it is plain, that every step in reasoning that produces knowledge, has intuitive certainty."[25]

Locke again adds in good Cartesian fashion, "These two, viz., intuition and demonstration. are the degrees of our knowledge; whatever comes short of one of these, with what assurance soever embraced, is but *faith* or *opinion*, but not knowledge, at least in all general truths."[26]

From the above passages of the Book IV of the *Essay*, it is clearly seen how Locke's conception of knowledge is Cartesian in its essence. According to Locke this knowledge is either intuitive, a direct perception of logical relations of the '2 plus 1 equals 3' type or the demonstrative, defined by Descartes as a chain of successive intuitions. "Again, the 'deduction' of the *Regulae* is indistinguishable from the 'demonstration' of the *Essay*, each being conceived as consisting of a connected chain of intuitions."[27] Even Woozley remarked, "His (Locke) account of intuition and demonstration is exactly the same as Descartes and shows clear evidence of the influence of the*Regulae*."[28]

If the above analysis of non-sensible sources of knowledge would found to be true in case of Locke, then it seems that Locke reached a crisis in his epistemological speculations. Because on the one hand, he propounded a rationalistic ideal of knowledge he found in Descartes and on the other hand was his loyalty to his doctrine of experience. But to avoid this crisis Locke maintained that we can have knowledge of general truths by no means except intuition and demonstration which resulted in acquisition of particular truths by an appeal to our senses and as a consequence of this he accepted the third degree of knowledge known as *sensitive knowledge*. But, acceptance of the third degree of knowledge in the form of sensitive, created a confusion within himself as well as commentators. First, when Locke stated that, "Intuition and demonstration, are the degrees of our knowledge; whatever comes short of one of these, with what assurance so far embraced, is but faith and opinion, but not knowledge, at least in all general truths,"[29] clearly shows the absence of 'appeal to sense! But subsequently being aware of inconsistency, it seems that Locke admitted the third degree of knowledge. Nevertheless, it leaves an impression that he was aware of inadequacy of sense-perception in construction of knowledge. Secondly, commentators like Morris remarked that, "It must be admitted that Locke's account of it (sensitive knowledge) is not very detailed or careful; perhaps because he thought it to be his business as a philosopher to give his attention primarily to knowledge proper."[30] Aaron writes, "The manner in which he introduces this third kind of knowledge reveals his uncertainty as to its precise nature,"[31] and continued further that, "Locke attempts to give further details of sensitive knowledge both in IV, ii, 14 and in IV, xi he speaks in the most uncertain tones."[32] The above considerations suggest that for Locke only intuitive and demonstrative degrees of knowledge constitute the criteria for the construction of knowledge, rather, in other words, the highest degree of knowledge for Locke is *intuition*, which he took over directly from Descartes.[33] The above views certainly reveal an inconsistency in Locke. But Aaron[34] tried to resolve this inconsistency and explained that Locke's teaching is identical with Descartes' as to the subjective side of the experience, but it is not so with regard to objective aspect. So far the object of intuition is concerned Locke is in conscious opposition to Descartes. Because for Descartes, object of intuition is pure and non-sensuous while for Locke it is sensuous. Therefore Aaron categorically maintained that for Locke intuitionism is only as part of his empiricism. If we accept this interpretation of Aaron, then what about his other explanations that, "Locke, it seems to me, owes his intuitionism to Descartes and in his description of intuition in IV, ii, 1 of the *Essay* he brings out this feature of Descartes' teaching very clearly."[35]

But the distinction between subjective and objective aspects of intuition can be objected to on the following grounds:

1. Firstly, it seems a confusion of *distinction* and *separation*. To claim that the object of intuition is distinct, therefore Locke is in conscious opposition to Descartes seems to involve a confusion regarding distinguishables as separables.[36]

2. Secondly, so far *intuition* is concerned it starts with *immediate apprehension* and in that immediacy whether the object of apprehension would be non-sensuous or sensuous, seems an unwanted question. Taking, both (1 &2) one can at least speak them as distinct, but to infer both as separate seems fallacious. Then the alternative would be, ***distinct but not separate***, in that case, the argument that, "Locke is in conscious opposition to Descartes," becomes questionable.

However, if we go into some details to the intuitionism of both Descartes and Locke, we find either directly or indirectly that Locke was influenced by Descartes. But Locke did not merely receive that, rather he rendered that more definite modified and developed in the new directions. But while doing so, Locke committed inconsistencies, because he could not make use of intuition in the Cartesian fashion,[37] because Locke put this theory of intuition in the context of his contention that knowledge goes only as far as experience is concerned. As a consequence of this, Locke could not use reason to leap beyond ideas in the mind to things outside of the mind.

(ii) Locke's Philosophy of Mind

The above discussion of intuition both in Descartes and Locke, amply suggests that Cartesian intuition is likely to be more stronger than that of Locke, I claim this supposition here on a consideration of Locke's philosophy of Mind. Because the conception of knowledge comes after a critical examination of Locke's epistemology requires a corresponding conception of mind but it seems Locke does not provide such an account. Locke started with the presupposition, that since man is born with no knowledge innate in him, the mind at birth must be a kind of *tabula rasa*, ready to receive impression, but not yet having received any.[38] Therefore, all the knowledge and all the beliefs which have been acquired by man, must be founded in the experience of the individual during their lives and not from any other source whatsoever. Since the mind does not possess the innate-ideas, Locke asserted, due to *sensation* and *reflection* the mind receives ideas. But in case of *reflection*, which are not sensible ideas, depend upon activities of *comparison* and *abstraction*, so that in the reception of them the mind cannot rightly be regarded as merely receiving sensations, which was presumed by Locke.

Once again, Locke claimed that which we think about, must be provided by some means other than thinking. Since he cannot admit innate principles, from which thinking may start, he adopted that it is provided by *simple ideas of sensations*. Further he asserted that the mind must be provided with ideas before it can think, since ideas do not come from thinking, therefore they necessarily come into the mind through the senses. If ideas come to the mind through senses prior to thought, then we must be able to detect their passage into the mind. This is what Locke was trying to do throughout with much confusion. The reason of this confusion might be due to lack of psychological clarity in him. Because having convinced that the ideas with which thought deals arise in the mind through sense-perception he should have supplied a careful analysis of sense-perception in order to distinguish *that of which we are immediately aware from that which we conclude from our immediate awareness*.

However, in emphasizing the role of experience in the construction of knowledge, Locke offered an important contribution, which the Cartesians failed to notice properly, but on the other hand his challenge became futile without any proper analysis. Therefore, Kant rightly saw, Locke's psychological method was not itself competent to achieve his critical aim.[39] But the fact remains that Lockes' doctrine of experience and Descartes adherence to doctrine of innate-ideas, very well supplied a solid background to Kant. Therefore in Kant we see, that the mind instead of being merely a *tabula rasa* of Locke ready and waiting to receive impressions, it is also gifted as part of its nature certain capacities to do something like that of Descartes.[40]

Both Locke and Descartes differ fundamentally as to the assumption that *thought is the essence of the mind* and *Extension is the essence of the body or material substance*.[41] Locke claimed on ontological level that to comprehend the nature of substance is too much for our understanding. He was right in arguing that we cannot think of qualities independently, there must be something in which they inhere. Further we do not think of an object as merely being the sum of its qualities, there must be something, which holds qualities together and marks the object an object, without this the qualities fall apart and cannot make a unity at all. And that something cannot be apprehended by sense, because that is not a quality. From this it follows that according to the principles of empirical philosophy, that cannot be apprehended at all. Therefore Locke, claimed a substance to be, "something he knew not what."[42] And moreover his polemic against the idea that soul always thinks is considered to be a fallacy of *ignoratio elenchi.*[43]

But coming to epistemology we see that for Locke, *sensation* and *reflection* constitute the whole material of our knowledge. What then is the role of *reflection*, if that does not help in knowing the essence of the substance or mind ? Because, Locke not only recognizes *reflection* but also in the end he found real adequate knowledge in the domain of reflective reason. Then, where does Locke stand ? To Descartes, mind being a substance maintains its identity, while to Hume, mind has no essence except a bundle or series of perceptions. If these views are two extremes, then what is the status of Locke's views on mind. This reveals atleast the instability so far as Locke's views on mind are concerned.

If the above observations regarding Locke's attack on innate principle and the corresponding philosophy of mind are to be accepted, then the traditionally accepted relation between Locke and Descartes in particular and empiricism and rationalism in general has to be modified. Here my suggestion would be that because of the confusion amongst historians, empiricism and rationalism has been accepted as two blocks having diametrically opposed views, otherwise not. If this would be discussed further it will reveal the following situation.

So far as the observations reveal Locke to be very much inadequate in his conception of empiricism because of his frequent adherence to strict rationalism which is specially apparent in *IV Book of his Essay* Now the controversy arose precisely to decide whether Locke is an empiricist or not. Locke is an empiricist with respect to the *Origin of Ideas* and also an empiricist in so far as he rejects *innate-ideas*, but he is not an empiricist with respect to the *question of knowledge.*

Because one fundamental conception in his theory of knowledge is that, the knowledge in general, truth can be acquired only by perceiving connections between the appropriate abstract ideas and therefore cannot be acquired by empirical means. (See IV, iii-31) (IV, vi-13) (IV. ix-1) (IV, xi-13-14), because he feels *the knowledge of general truths must be the knowledge of necessary truth.* He accepts the knowledge of general truth to be solely a matter of perceiving connections between ideas, because it is the knowledge of essences and of eternal truth (Iv, iii-31), consequently, he claims that some our knowledge are acquired by non-empirical means and that all our general knowledge must be acquired by such means. Indeed, to the extent that he restricts knowledge of general truth to the knowledge of necessary truth, he can said to manifest a form of rationalism. Being a strict empiricist he cannot admit knowledge of necessary truths. The only necessary truth for an expiricist would be tautologies. Once again, so far his views on necessary truth and the knowledge of necessary truth are concerned, he can for the most part be called a rationalist. Because he allows for the existence of necessary non-identical truths in the areas of Natural Science and Metaphysics, although such truths are largely beyond human powers of perception. Secondly, he admits the possibility of non-identical, and non-formal necessary truths and thirdly, he does not seek to reduce the knowledge of necessary truths to the knowledge of linguistic facts. Further knowledge of necessary truths like; Laws of Nature, existence of independent objects, that there are real objects independent of sense-experience, existence of mind and substance, to sense-experience. These led him to claim that such knowledge derived by non-empirical means. Then the obvious question is, what is that non-empirical source of knowledge ? To Locke, it must be due to intuition, which he has accepted as the source of certainty of knowledge and this acceptance of intuition suggests an innatism in the form of innate faculty, which Locke has accepted. Therefore Sorely rightly speaks with regard to Locke that "The mind has no innate-ideas, but it has innate faculties. . . ."[44] Which means otherwise the mind which is endowed with reason has a capacity to intuit the connections of ideas and as a result of that we do derive the knowledge of necessary truths.

If á comparison is to be drawn here between empiricism and rationalism, taking the above views of Locke into consideration, we see that, common pre-suppositions of both empiricism and rationalism of 17th and 18th century was that philosophy requires a method and these two schools differed, if in nothing else,. but only regarding the nature of that method.[45] They differed about how certainty was to be attained. They differed also in their conception of the extent to which the ideas in terms of which knowledge is to be formulated are derived from the use of our *senses.* as opposed to the use of *reason.* It should be added however that these differences are differences of *tendency*[46] only. In a sense, to talk of opposing *schools* of philosophy is misleading. Because, there is much in Descartes, that would by certain criteria make him an empiricist, and there is similarly much in Locke that would make him a rationalist. But they exhibit tendencies in opposite direction. Rationalists tended to appeal to reason as the source of knowledge and of some ideas atleast, while empiricists tended to depreciate reason as a source of knowledge and insist that all ideas come from experience. The rationalists view of mind tended to be that of a substance engaging in cognitive activity, while the empiricists tended to take a passive view of the mind and to eschew the notion of substances. And the issue between empiricists and rationalists over the genesis of our ideas can be said to be misplaced. In so far as it is strictly a question about the *genesis* of those ideas it belongs to the province of psychology. In so far as it is a question about the *logical character* of those ideas seems to be too complex to be dealt with by a simple minded espousal of rationalism or empiricism.[47]

To sum up, the views of Locke presented in Book I of the *Essays* regarding rejection of innate principles and the views of Book IV regarding acceptance of non-empirical sources of knowledge like intuition, put Locke in between empiricism and rationalism. Therefore, his outright rejection of innate principles and ideas in Book I seems to be philosophically insignificant. And his deliberations in Book IV of the *Essay* seems quite significant; because whenever possible he followed Descartes to the maximum. Therefore, Yolton has rightly remarked that Locke's construction of general knowledge is like Descartes' in nature, once the materials are available.[48]

REFERENCES

1. The 1st Book of the *Essay* is devoted to this polemic. My reference would be A. C. Fraser's Vol. I and Vol. II Dover Publications, 1959.
2. Book I, p. 37.
3. *Appendix B*, may be confered for the search which has been undertaken.
4. Aaron, *John Locke*, (Oxford, 1955).
5. Leibniz connected the polemic with the Cartesians in 1996 in his first short paper on Locke's Essay. *New Essays C. H. U.* Translated by Langley (Open Court Publishing Company, 1916).
6. In his letter on Locke in the *Lettres Philosophiques*.
7. Aaron, *John Locke*, p. 90.
8. Book I, p. 37.
9. Ibid., p. 39.
10. Ibid., p. 40.
11. Ibid., p. 45.
12. Cf. Book I, pp. 62-64.
13. Book I.. pp. 38-39.
14. Cf., James Gibson, *Locke's Theory of Knowledge.*, Cambridge, At University Press, 1968, p. 38.
15. Cf., Ibid., p. 39.
16. Third letter to Stilling fleet, Works Vol. VI. p. 459 (Cf., Op. cit., *Lockes Theory of Knowledge*, James Gibson, p. 209).
17. Essay, The Epistle to the Reader. (Cf. Op. cit., *Locke's Theory of Knowledge*, James Gibson, p. 209).
18. Book IV, 1.2. p. 167.
19. Ibid., 2.1. p. 176.
20. Ibid., p. 177.
21. Ibid., 2, 14. p. 185.
22. Op. cit., *Regulae* III.
23. Regarding Locke's acquaintance with the work *Regulae*, the possibilities have already been suggested, need not be mentioned here, for reference, please see, Op. cit., Gibson—*Locke's Theory of Knowledge*—pp. 211-12, Op. cit., Aaron, *John Locke*, pp. 220-21.
24. Book IV, p. 178.
25. Ibid., pp. 180-81.
26. Ibid., p. 185.
27. Op. cit, Gibson, p. 212.
28. A. D. Woozley; (ed.) *John Locke An Essay Concerning Human Understanding*; Fontana, 1975, p. 46.
29. Book IV., p. 185.
30. C. R. Morris, *Locke, Berkeley, Hume*, Oxford, 1931. p. 48.
31. Aaron, *John Locke*, p. 245.
32. Ibid., p. 245.

33. Cf., Lamprecht, *Our Philosophical traditions*, p. 308. (Appleton-Century-Crofts, INC. 1955).
34. Cf., Aaron., *John Locke*. p. 224.
35. Aaron, *Knowing and the Function of Reason*, Oxford. 1971 For further clarification regarding this feature of Descartes' teaching—please confer pp. 31-32.
36. S. S. Barlingay, *I. P. Q.* Jan. 1975, Vol. II, "Distinguishables and Separables."
37. Cf., Op. cit., Lamprecht, *Our Philosophical Traditions*, p. 308.
38. Cf. Book II, i.2. pp. 121-22.
39. Cf., Op. cit., Morris, C. R., p. 25.
40. This is discussed on a Chapter on Kant.
41. For detailed account please refer, Op. cit., Gibson, *Locke's Theory of Knowledge*, pp. 217-22.
42. Essay, Book II, XXIII, 2., p. 392.
43. G. E. M. Anscombe and P. Geach, ed., *Descartes Philosophical Writings*, (London, 1975). (Cf. "Perception and immortality in the Nouveaux Essais", Nicholas Jolley, *Journal of the History of Philosophy*, April 1978, Vol. XVI, No. 2., p. 189.
44. W. R. Sorley, *A History of British Philosophy to 1900* pp. 112-13. (Cambridge, 1965).
45. Descartes believed in method of geometry and British Empiricists influenced by the results of Newton's inquiry.
46. Cf. Hamlyn, *Sensations and Perception*, pp. 55-59. Routledge and Kegan Paul, London, 1961.
47. Ibid., p. 60.*

*If we accept the difference between empiricism and rationalism as a matter of *tendency*, then it would reveal that the difference between both, may be philosophically insignificant. Because the empiricists always attacked rationalism by the argument that the rationalists neglect the contribution of sense observation to knowledge. But in developing their own philosophy, the empiricists unconsciously accepted the fundamental thesis of rationalism. Therefore it has been rightly remarked that the *tug-of-war* between the two *lacks a rope*, (*The Concise Encyclopaedia of Western Philosophy and Philosophers*, ed. J. O. Urmson, London, 1960). Particularly in Descartes and Locke as we have seen their approach towards epistemology was not opposed to each other. To quote Gibson here, "so freely, indeed, does he transform the Cartesian principles, that the existence of any positive relation of dependence upon them has frequently been ignored by the historian of philosophy, and the position of Descartes and Locke have been set in antithetical opposition to each other (Gibson, *John Locke's Theory of Knowledge*, p. 207). And the confusion which has been raised by the traditional thinkers would get a further blow if a proper notice would be given to Lamprecht.

"Descartes on the continent and Locke in England, different as their views were in other respects, agreed in regarding the Content of sense experience as an inadequate basis for knowledge of the real World. Descartes then defended the power of the mind to reach clear and distinct ideas, by means of which reason could surmount the limitations of sense; and Locke sought to reconcile himself to the agnostic implications of those same limitations. But in Descartes and Locke alike, sense experience was a succession of ideas which could not be taken to indicate the real nature of the external bodies which produce those ideas in human minds. In Descartes and Locke alike, there appeared a contrast between experience (which may be called subjective because it inheres in private minds) and nature (which may be called objective because it exists apart from private minds)" (Our Philosophical Traditions, p. 313).

48. Cf. John Yolton., ed., *An Essay Concerning Human Understanding*, London. 1961. pp. xix-xx.

Note: Appendix C, which deals with Leibniz-Locke controversy on innate-ideas may please be considered as a part of the debate.

6

The Transformation of the Problem in Kant's Critical Philosophy: The Foundations of a Meta-Theory of Innateness

(i) The Task of Critical Philosophy

For the sake of convenience, I would divide my discussion of Kant into negative and positive aspects. In the negative part, I would throw light upon Kant's criticism of both Dogmatism and Scepticism with particular reference to Descartes and Locke. First of all I hope to study Kant's criticism of the epistemology of Descartes and Locke. Next my concern would be to deduce the epistemological assumptions of Kant from his criticism. The positive aspect would be a discussion of Kant's Copernican Revolution and its relevant epistemological implications. Then I would deal with how Kant has shifted the domain of philosophy from ordinary or empirical discourse to a discourse of transcendentalism in order to ensure epistemology as a whole. Through out the discussion my purpose would be to see how his contribution to major philosophical advances in epistemology in general and the philosophy of mind in particular remains as the landmark in the history of philosophy.

Before dealing with the criticism of the *Problematic idealism* of Descartes and the *physiology of knowledge* of Locke, let us see first the pre-critical period of Kant and its influence on him which leads him to his critical philosophy.

Kant in his so-called pre-critical period has accepted Hume's argument and convinced himself that to deal with metaphysics was to waste time, which has been expressed in the "Dreams of Ghost-Seer, elucidated by Dreams of Metaphysics" (1766). Even after his idea of critical philosophy, he remained an admirer of Hume but held that to be engaged in metaphysical inquiry one must be clear about the nature, the logical status and the method of acceptability of metaphysical propositions. He clarified further that before indulging in metaphysics we need a critique of reason to show how far or in what sense it is a possibility, which he presented in "Prolegomen to any Future Metaphysic which is to rank as Science,' (1783). To Hume and to Logical positivists, metaphysical propositions are neither empirical nor analytic, because they are neither verifiable nor their denials are self contradictory, further they also claim that those propositions are meaningless. On the other hand, the empiricism of Hume led him with the logical necessity to a form of scepticism having disastrous consequences for our view of understanding of reality and Kant's main target is an attempt to overcome this scepticism of Hume. It is not only that Hume interrupted Kant's dogmatic slumbers which has been quoted often; one should also notice at the same time the influence of Leibniz upon him. In the 1768 there appeared Duten's edition of Leibniz's writings containing the Leibniz-Clarke correspondence, before this Kant was in touch of Leibniz through the medium of the Wolffian philosophy, which appeared in his inaugural dissertation as professor, "On the Forms and Principles of the sensible and Intelligible world," (1770). To start with, we find that Kant accepted the view of Leibniz's that space and time are phenomenal and they are not properties of things-in-themselves. But Kant did not accept Leibniz's notion that they are confused ideas or representations, for in that case geometary would not be the exact science which it is. Therefore Kant speaks of space and time as "pure intuitions". To make this point intelligible, one should go back to his inaugural dissertation where he divides human knowledge into sensitive and intellectual and the world into sensible and intelligible. This naturally suggests that intelletual knowledge is knowledge of intelligiblia just as sensitive knowledge is knowledge of sensiblia. This two-fold scheme of knowledge and of objects of knowledge proposed under the influence of Leibniz made it difficult for Kant to throw dogmatic metaphysics away.

With this background, if one wants to study the actual epistemological assumptions of Kant then going through the *Critique of Pure Reason* is a must, because the theory of knowledge which is very significant in Kant's philosophy is set forth there only. The first edition of the critique appeared 1781 and the second edition in its improved version was published in 1787. In this *Critique of Pure Reason* Kant attempts among other things, to establish the validity of knowledge and the impossibility of metaphysics.

So far as Hume is concerned, Kant does not accept the dichotomy of empirical any analytic proposition, because he believes that we are in possession of propositions which fall into none of the above categories. The other class of propositions, are the synthetic a priori whose logical nature, function and systematic connection with each other and with other types of propositions is the main topic of his philosophy. Kant's classification is not of propositions but of judgments (i.e. regarding propositions asserted by somebody). Every judgment according to Kant is either analytic or synthetic. "In all judgments in which the relation of a subject to the predicate is thought. . . this relation is possible in two different ways. Either the predicate B belongs to the subject A, as something which is (covertly) contained in this concept A; or B lies outside the concept A, although it does indeed stand in connection with it. In the one case I entitle the judgment analytic, in the other synthetic" (B 10).[1] Again Kant asserted that a judgment is either a priori or a posteriori. A judgment is a priori, "if it is independent of all experience and even of all impressions of the senses," (B2). And judgments which are not *a priori* are a posteriori, i.e. they depend logically on other judgments which describe experiences or impressions of the senses. Taking both the above classifications into consideration, we can find that Kant admits four possibilities :

1. Synthetic a posteriori
2. Synthetic a priori
3. Analytic a priori and
4. Analytic a posteriori.

Form this classification the fourth possibility must be ruled out, because there can be no analytic a posteriori judgments. Regarding other three possibilities Kant holds that they are not only possible but are frequently examplified in our thinking. The analytic judgments must be a priori since they merely elucidate the meaning of their terms and therefore are logically independent of judgments describing sense-experience. If analytic judgments are necessarily a priori then all that are a posteriori (non-analytic) are necessarily synthetic (non-analytic).

The remaining possibility is that of synthetic a priori judgment whose predicates are not contained in their subjects and yet are logically independent of all judgments describing sense-experience. Kant holds this type of synthetic a priori judgments are found in mathematics and physics. Kant raises the question whether the synthetic a priori judgments are found in metaphysics or not ? To Kant metaphysics which makes assertions beyond the realm of experience, at the same time which employs concepts whose significance borrowed from sense-experience, in consequence of which justification for their being used outside of this realm can be called into question. And precisely, Kant says, here lies the possibility of synthetic a priori propositions in meta-physics. After stating this, Kant formulates his basic problems: How are synthetic a priori judgments possible ? To answer this question is also to answer the following questions :

1. How are synthetic a priori judgments in Meta-physics possible ? and
2. How are synthetic a priori judgments in Physics possible ?

Kant answered the first question in the *Transcendental Aesthetic* and the second on in the *Transcendental Analytic.*

This problem of synthetic a priori judgments depend on

Kant's general view of judging or thinking. One of his fundamental assumptions is that judging and perceiving are irreducibly different. In this Kant was opposed to both rationalists and empiricists. To rationalists perceiving was a kind of low-grade judging while empiricists inclined to assimilate judging to perceiving. Kant expressed this sharp distinction between judging and perceiving as one between two distinct faculties of mind, i.e. understanding and sense. "By means of sense objects are given to us and sense alone provides us with perception; by means of the understanding objects are thought and from it there it arise concepts," (B 33). The sense is the faculty of apprehending particulars which are given in space and time or both and of apprehending space and time themselves which are also particulars. To Kant the notions of space and time are not abstractions from perceptions but a priori particulars or "pure forms of perceptions." The understanding is the faculty of recognition through concepts which refer to sense given particulars, these concepts are either a posteriori or a priori. To Kant the general notions which are neither abstracted from perceptions nor applicable to it are ideas. The faculty of employing ideas is called reason, which covers both understanding and pure forms of perception.

(ii) The Refutation of Problematic Idealism

Keeping in mind further connected philosophical assumptions for the time being here, let us see how Kant attacks the *problematic idealism* of Descartes and *physiology of knowledge* of Locke respectively. Particularly I would discuss Descartes and Locke in this context because I have already considered their views taking both as pioneer of rationalism and empiricism respectively.

Both editions of the *Critique of Pure Reason* contain a refutation of idealism[2] but in second edition particularly the term "problematic idealism" occurs.

"Idealism—meaning thereby *material* idealism—is the theory which declares the existence of objects in space outside us either to be merely doubtful and indemonstrable or to be false and impossible. The former is the *problematic* idealism of Descartes, which holds that there is only one empirical assertion that is indubitably certain, namely, that 'I am'. The latter is the *dogmatic* idealism of Berkeley" (B 274).

Kant has overthrown the dogmatic idealism in the *Transcendental Aesthetic* and refused only the empirical idealism of Descartes which Kant later on came to call "material or problematic idealism" in the second edition of the Critique. The *problematic idealism* of Descartes consists that only our own existence and inner states are immediately apprehended by us, all perceptions are modifications of our inner-sense, and the existence of external objects can therefore be asserted only by an inference. This idealism of Descartes with its conception of the problematic status of the external world is seen to be a consequence of the primacy of *Cogito*. The decisive feature of this doctrine is the epistemic priority which it grants to inner over outer experience. One's own existence and conscious states are held to be the sole objects of direct acquintance and the existence of the external objects are only to be assertained by means of causal inference.

In order to refute the above form of idealism, Kant employed the thesis that the empirically determined consciousness of my own existence proves the existence of objects in space out side me, which means, I am conscious of my own existence as determined in time. But all determination in time pre-supposes the existence of something permanent in perception. But this something permanent can not be intuitable in the empirical self. For it is the condition of my existence in time. Therefore it follows that the perception of my own existence in time is possible only through the existence of something real outside me. Consciousness in time is thus necessarily connected with the existence of external things not merely with the representation of things external to me. In other words one becomes conscious of himself in perceiving external things.[3] The question of inferring the existence of external things does not arise.

The problem of the external world which emerges here needs a further clarification. Kant said, "It always remains doubtful whether the cause be internal or external; whether, that is to say, all the so called outer perceptions are not a mere play of our inner sense, or whether they stand in relation to actual external objects as their cause," (A 368). This is the classical formulation of the problem of the external world. Kant's aim is to show that it as a pseudo-problem, because this arises from false metaphysical assumptions. Kant calls this assumption as *transcendental realism* and he opposes it to his *transcendental idealism.* The defining characteristic of *transcendental realism* is its confusion of appearance with things-in-themselves. Proponents of this *transcendental realism*, Descartes and Newton, regarded, "Time and space as something given themselves, independently of our sensibility" (A 369). As a consequence of this erroneous conception of space and time they treat objects in space and time as things-in-themselves. This view of space and time gives rise in these thinkers to a conception of reality or nature as composed of bodies containing only primary and secondary qualities.

Kant's main contention was that it is the misguided realism which give rise to the equally misguided idealism of the Cartesian School. Because the assumption that physical objects exist independently of the mind, the transcendental realists, "finds that, judged from this point of view, all our sensuous representations are inadequate to establish their reality" (A 369). Here Kant reveals an insight into the connection between the metaphysical conception of nature developed by the science and the Cartesian—Lockean theory of ideas, i.e., the theory that ideas or sensations are the immediate objects of consciousness. Transcendental realists define the nature of reality in such a way that it remains totally inaccessible to consciousness, thus it is unable to justify the validity of its conception. This leads to an *empirical idealism* that what are accessible to consciousness are only its own private and subjective modifications, i.e., the Cartesian ideas and sensations. It is no doubt with this in mind that Kant concludes, "If we treat outer objects as things in themselves, it is quite impossible to understand how we could arrive at a knowledge of their reality outside us, since we have to rely merely on the representation which is in us." (A 378).

In opposition to this view and to scepticism, Kant offers his own doctrine of *transcendental idealism* which he claimed to have established in the *Transcendental Aesthetic.* That is defined as, "the doctrine that appearances are to be regarded as being, one and all, representations only, not things in themselves." (369 A).

Thus Kant resolves the problem of the external world by showing that the external world in question is not external in the sense in which *transcendental realism* believed. He can therefore maintain that his experience of a world of bodies in space is as immediate and veridical as the experience of his own subjective states. This is possible because he regards space and time as forms of human sensibility rather than as things-in-themselves. So that both they and the things in them are not external in the transcendental sense.

Descartes' approach was wrong for he assumes that we possess consciousness of our selves independent of and prior to experience of external things; then questions arise how the ego, certain of its own existence, can know that there are external things. Especially Descartes' distinction of objective independently real and subjective as the field of consciousness, became his wrong articulation. Kant reacts to this and says that all subjectivist modes of starting the problem of knowledge, which includes the view of Hume, Leibniz, Descartes, Locke, and Berkeley are illigitimate and question begging. He continued further, that the subjective is not to be regarded as opposite in nature but a sub-species within it. Therefore Kant states, that the problem of knowledge is not how we can advance from the merely subjective to knowledge of the independently real, that is to say, objective, but how consciousness and the complex factors which contribute to its possibility are to be interpreted. As a consequence, Kant abondoned both subjectivism and materialism but adopted a non-committal attitude. The position of Kant here can be explained as follows; to eliminate subjectivism is not maintain the illusory or the phenomenal character of the individual self and to rule out materialism is not to assert that the unconscious may not generate and account for the conscious. Ultimately this Cartesian dualism of subjective and objective is thus subordinated to the critical distinction between appearance and reality of Kant. This confusion regarding appearance and reality arises precisely in case of Descartes and others, Kant says, because they confuse external objects with things-in-themselves. For Kant "external" has got both empirical and transcendental meaning. To be external in empirical sense is to be in space and to which the categories are applicable while in the transcendental sense, it is entirely free from sensibility and can not be explained by reference to space. Similarly Kant also gives both an empirical and transcendental meaning of "appearance". For him, appearance empirically means, that which covers things that are spatial, belonging to inner-sense, such as sensation, while transcendentally it means, appearances are not things-in-themselves. Kant makes it clear that empirical and transcendental, should understood to refer not to two different kinds of entity, but instead to two different ways of talking about one and the same thing.

This account of Kant's distinction between empirical and transcendental enables us to estimate Kant's account of perception and also to resolve the problem that arises from the notion of appearance. The epistemological assumptions deduced from above refutation of *problematic idealism*, which leads to the distinction of inner and outer, appearance and things-in-themselves is clearly connected with the contrast between sense and understanding. In the *Critique of Pure Reason*, therefore it is remarked that, "The division of objects into phenomena and noumena and the world into a world of senses and a world of understanding, is therefore quite inadmissible in the positive sense, although the distinction of concepts as sensible or intellectual is certainly legitimate", (11 B). It is also held further in (62 B) that the contrast between the two faculties is not a logical but transcendental distinction. For to deny the contrast was merely logical for Kant, to deny the dogmatic view that the understanding gave us knowledge of intelligible objects. Kant admitted the existence of an intelligible contribution to knowledge but on the other hand denied that this provided knowledge of any intelligible objects. The knowledge of intelligible objects can only be obtained by the co-operation of both sense and understanding. Therefore from the refutation of Descartes' *problematic idealism,* Kant arrived at a new account of the conception of mind. In the case of Descartes the mind was only aware of inner and subjective states by means of its own understanding without recognising the outer, that is to say external objects. But Kant's analysis presupposes that the mind is not only aware of outer objects directly but that makes awareness of inner-sensation possible. Therefore to Kant the mind needs both sensibility and understanding and their nature is such that in isolation of one the other is useless.

(iii) Critique of Locke's Physiology of the Human Understanding

Works of both Locke's *Essay* and Kant's *Critique of Pure Reason* contain the record of an intellectual development, because two thinkers are seeking to approach the problems of philosophy from a new angle. However Kant's achievements remain as an advance upon Locke. Because Kant's method was the method of transcendental philosophy, and he also proposed to survey the field of human knowledge as Locke has done; but from an entirely different point of view. Kant was interested not in knowledge as such that is *physiology of knowledge* but in *a priori knowledge*. He proposed to discover and examine the validity of just those concepts of which he believed the empiricism had no satisfactory answer to offer.

Kant recognised two distinct questions which can be asked about concepts. The first is a question of fact (*quid facti*) and the other question is a question of right (*quid juris*).[4] The question of fact amounts to, "how do we come to have the concepts, and what is involved in our having it?" Kant calls this the *Physiology of human understanding* which was practised by Locke.[5] To explain, Locke in his theory of perception advocated that objects are reflected through a lens (the retina) into a dark room (the interior of the skull) whese we must suppose that the appearances (ideas) of them are literally thrown on to a clean state (tabula rasa). Locke through this kind of operation of the human mind wants to discover the matters where we may hope for certainly and also matters where we have to remain content with opinion and conjecture. But according to Kant, it becomes quite inadequate to serve its intended purpose, because it does not probe deeply enough and remains limited by its empirical approach. Therefore Kant comments, "The illustrious Locke, falling to take account of these considerations, (see the need to validate the pure concepts of the understanding as a priori conditions of the possibility of experience), and meeting with pure concepts of the understanding in experience, deduced then also from experience, and yet proceeded so *inconsequently* that he attempted with their aid to obtain knowledge which far transcends all limits of experience." (127 B).

Kant's second question is the question of right, which aims at the right or justification for the possession and employment of those concepts. Kant clarified here that although concepts can be derived from experience by various means they might still lack objective validity and to show that this is not so is the task of *the Transcendental deduction*

Kant tried hard to avoid the misleading features of his terminology by explicitly distinguishing his task from that which he believed Locke to have undertaken. In passage (118B—20) Kant distinguishes between an empirical inquiry into the origin of ideas, such as Locke's and a transcendental inquiry into the status of concepts, such as his own. The main task of Kant is to show explicity that the *Critique* is not concerned with the aims or methods of empirical psychology, which was primarily Locke's concern. A similar distinction Kant made in (A 97) the 1st edition deduction, where Kant introduces the three-fold synthesis. Once again Kant rejects the empirical and chooses the transcendental inquiry. In this distinction but one thing becomes certain that Kant firmly rejected the claim that he was engaged in empirical investigation into the origin of ideas, which was the concern of "the celebrated Locke". In the Prolegomena (Sect 21a, AK, Vol. 4, Bo4), Kant also says, "To put all this in a nutshell, it is first necessary to remind the reader that we are not here talking of the origin of experience but of what is in it. The former task belongs to empirical psychology and would never be able to be developed but for the latter, which belongs to a critique of knowledge and especially of the understanding."

From the above illustrations it becomes clear how Kant reacted to the natural analysis of knowledge undertaken by Locke. Kant's contention was that Lockes' account of experience was not final. Locke only aims at empirical derivations of ideas and its origin overlooking the vital aspect, that is to say cooperation of the senses with understanding which aims at justification.

From the Refutation of ***Problematic Idealism***, it is learnt that Descartes' epistemology overlooked the significance of sensation for the construction of knowledge, rather he deduced judgments concerning reality from concepts alone without relying on sensation. On the other hand, from the ***physiology of human understanding***, it is learnt that the question of right or justification regarding the employment of concepts are primary over the question of fact. And this justification in case of epistemology can only be achieved through the deduction of categories from the pure understanding.

The rationalistic tradition, has, intellectualised the appearances and the Lockean tradition, have sensualised all the concepts of intellect. "In a word, Leibniz *intellectualised* appearances, just as Locke, according to his system of *noogony*, *sensualised* all concepts of the understanding, i.e., interpreted them as nothing more than empirical or abstracted concepts of reflection." (A 271—B 327).

(iv) The Transcendental Solution

For Kant, the task is to break the coalition with due regard to both the groups. Having this as back ground Kant operates with the *Ramsey's Maxim*[6] which means that the truth lies not in one of the two but in some third possibility, which can be discovered rejecting something assumed as obvious by both the disputants, in order to resolve the controversy. And subsequently the result of this debate appeared in the form of the *Copernican Revolution*[7] in Kant. Kant compares his epistemology to the *Copernican hypothesis.* The predecessors of Copernicus had difficulty in explaining the apparent notions of the planets on the supposition that they all revolve around the earth. Before Kant, it was similarly impossible in philosophy to explain how there would be a priori knowledge of things on the assumption that knowledge is a passive conformity to the objects. "Failing of satisfactory progress in explaining the movement of the heavenly bodies on the supposition that they all revolve round the spectator." Kant says, "he (Copernicus) tried whether he might not have better success if he made the spectator to revolve and the stars to remain at rest" (B XVI). Similarly, if the phenomenal characteristics of objects are explained in terms of the behaviour of the knowing mind, it is possible to see how the knowledge of them can be a priori, for to be an object of knowledge, they must conform to the structure and activity of the knowing mind which make knowledge possible. Or to explain it in other words, Kant assumes that the human mind is the centre of the phenomenal universe, so that things must conform to our mind, rather than our mind to things. This sort of explanation of Kant certainly gives a leverage to the rationalistic method. Because while empiricism had to stop at the limits of sense-experience, rationalism was perhaps even more fruitful beyond these boundaries. But after that Kant discovered that rationalistic method accomplished too much, it not only proved the thesis which transcend possible experience; with equal force it proved their antithesis too. Therefore Kant's epistemology ultimately driven to a situation which speaks, "Thoughts without content are empty intuitions without concepts are blind" (A 51—B 75). On the other hand, Kant's epistemology aims at combinations of both thought and intuition or faculty of understanding and faculty of sensibility. Neither alone cannot give us knowledge, either alone is blind or empty.

The above observations reveal that for Kant knowledge or experience requires both intuitions and concepts. The *Transcendental Aesthetic* examined a priori contributions to experience that is the faculty of intuition, and the *Transcendental Analytic* examines the a priori contributions of understanding, that is the faculty of concepts. Just as the *Transcendental Aesthetic* yielded pure-intuitions, space and the similarly the *Analytic* is to yield pure concepts of categories. The *Transcendental Analytic* was subdivided into *Analytic of concepts* and *Analytic of principles*. The *Analytic of concepts* demonstrates the possibility and necessity of concepts for experience which leads to a discussion of transcendental deduction of categories. On the other hand the *Analytic of principles* studies the rules applicable to experience. It contains the schematism of the categories and principles of pure understanding. First, let us start with the *Analytic of concepts*. According to Kant, there are twelve a priori categories of understanding.[8] But what is the justification for their employment in synthesising phenomena? What is the justification for their application to objects? Such a problem does not arise regarding the employment of the a priori forms of sensibility. But the situation regarding the categories of the understanding is different. Because the objects given in sense intuitions which are nothing but appearances; but if the categories of understanding would be applied to them, they may distort or misrepresent them. And the legitimacy of applying the categories to objects is task of the *Transcendental Deduction* which is different from the *Empirical Deduction*. To distinguish these two in detail, we find that Kant assumes that in human knowledge there are concepts, such as cause and effect, which are a priori, that is to say used independently of experience. Such use cannot be justified by an appeal to experience, because experience can never give us that universality and necessity which are the criteria of the a priori. In order to justify this we must explain how they can be related to objects which are not obtained from any experience, "they must be in a position to show a certificate of birth quite other than that of descent from experience" (A 86). Their justification cannot be found by the method used by Locke. Therefore the *transcendental deduction* finds the origin of concepts in the natural mind itself, and for that only can establish their objective validity, while the empirical deduction examines our method of acquiring concepts or how concepts are acquired by experience and by reflection upon experience. Here to follow Kant properly one must distinguish between the *origin* and *acquisition* of concepts. According to Kant, study of latter belongs properly to empirical psychology. Therefore the *transcendental deduction* is not however a question of *quid facti*, but of *quid juris*. It is not how extensively we employ categories but a question of whether our use of categories is legitimate or a necessary condition of knowledge. This line of thought clearly is involved in Kant's *Copernican Revolution*. The use of categories cannot be justified on the assumption that the mind must conform to objects. But if the objects to be known, must conform to the mind and if this means that they must be subjected to the categories of understanding in order to be objects, then no further justification of the use of categories is required.

The *transcendental deduction* is discussed in both the editions of the *Critique of Pure Reason*.[9] In the 1st edition, Kant gives a psychologically ariented explanation, which he calls *subjective deduction* of the nature of synthesis otherwise known as *metaphysical* deduction. The synthesis combines the manifold of sense impressions into a unity through principles of *apprehension, reproduction* and *recognition*. These are three aspects of one and the same process. These are necessary conditions of knowing an object. Kant says this sort of synthesis is not empirical but *a priori*. Without such a synthesis there would be no self-consciousness or even consciousness and therefore no experience. Hence, the concept object reflects the unity of consciousness. This unity is not empirically ascertained but is established *a priori*. This *unity of conscionsness* is consequently a transcendental condition, which Kant calls the *transcendental apperception.*

In the Second Edition of the *Critique* little is said about the synthesis of the manifold. It has already been considered as an established fact, that such a synthesis exists not as something given in sensation but as the result of the activity of the understanding, that is as the result of use of concepts. Further it is said, that by means of concepts, the judgments are possible and the judgments are necessary conditions of knowledge. Therefore the categories are necessary conditions of knowledge. Then the obvious question comes out, as how to apply the categories or concepts of the understanding to appearances? This has been answered by Kant in the *Analytic of Principles*. To Kant, the categories are not to be intuited, nor are they contained in appearances, how then can intuitions be subsumed under categories or pure concepts applicable to appearances. Kant's argument is, since categories and appearances are not homogeneous, a third thing is necessary. That third thing must be in one respect intelligible therefore similar to the categories and in another be sensible therefore similar to the intuitions to be conceptualised, which Kant calls *transcendental schema* (A 138-9/B 177-8). By schematising categories, by giving them a temporal interpretation, we obtain concepts that can find application in experience.

From the above it appears that Kant needs two notions to explain the possible conditions of human experience, one is intuition, given in space and time and the other is application of categories to what is given in intuition. Neither intuition alone nor categories alone can give knowledge. The categories are therefore necessary conditions of empirical knowledge, what Kant calls experience (B 147-48).

We have seen in the above how the trend of Kant's philosophy started with a *transcendental investigation.* Kant's primary aim of the *Critique of Pure Reason* from beginning to the end, is not to give a theory of knowledge or a theory of experience but to resolve this problem. The problem before him was, how is metaphysics possible as a science or to put it otherwise, how metaphysical knowledge is possible? In the *Critique*, Kant claims to have furnished the complete outline of the system for metaphysics. The main concern of Kant in the *Critique*, besides other relevant issues, is primarily, how can metaphysical judgments be verified? He started the investigation with the argument that metaphysical judgments are a priori and synthetic and the attempt to verify synthetic a priori judgments Kant calls a *transcendental investigation.* This notion of *transcendental investigation* arises because Kant played the role of a *Critique* whose function is not to extend, but only to clarify our reasons, and keep it free from errors (A 12). As a critique, Kant prescribed two routes for the *transcedental investigation*; they are *Transcendental Logic* and *Transcendental Aesthetic.* The *transcendental logic* has to do with judgments, with concepts and with the intellect, that is the faculty of thinking, while the *Transcendental Aesthetic* deals with observation and with the senses by which observation takes place. In the *Transcendental Aesthetic*, Kant does not propose an investigation of how man's sensory organs function or of how sensations arise. If it were that, it would verify its results only by recourse to observation and the principles which it reached would be empirical. Similarly in the *Transcendental Logic*, Kant does not propose an investigation of how all men always think. If it were so, it would be a part of psychology and could not establish any results a priori. Therefore Kant argues, both Locke and Hume, failed to ascertain whether or how metaphysical knowledge is possible, just because they tried to settle this by a psychological method, which leads to an empirical investigation (Cf. B 127 H). To make his role very much clearer, Kant means by the *Transcendental Aesthetic* an investigation generally seeks the conditions of obtaining observations, while the *Transcendental Logic* seeks the conditions of obtaining knowledge of any objects. Kant claims further that, if the *Transcendental Aesthetic* and the *Transcendental Logic* are to succeed in finding how synthetic judgments a priori can be verified, they must, like formal Logic, be independent of other principles, they should not make any psychological, biological or physical presuppositions. Here Kant's pertinent claim is the inadequacy of the psychological method for the solution of philosophical problems. To put it otherwise Kant separated the question of the origin and the actual development of man's activities, from those which relate to their validity. However, how far this total separation is possible becomes a debatable point with which I would be concerned later on.

(v) The Structure of Transcendental Arguments

The *Critique of Pure Reason* is called a Critique because it aims at a preliminary account of what reason can and cannot attempt in the way of a priori metaphysical speculations. It purports to settle the vital methodological problem concerning to Critique of knowledge before attempting to solve any specific philosophical dispute. Therefore, the *Critique of Pure Reason* has become a special science to Kant which contains the principles by which we know things absolutely a priori (A 11/B 25). The knowledge derived out of this science, Kant entitled *transcendental knowledge*, the system of such concepts entitled *transcendental philosophy*, the inquiry involved called *transcendental inquiry*, the arguments taken to proceed in the same inquiry are known as *transcendental arguments* and finally the method employed is called *transcendental method.* All the transcendental assumptions taken together form an organic whole. This organic nature is such that every part depends upon the adequate treatment of any other part. To change even a smallest part of it would give rise contradictions, not only in the system but in the human reason itself.

From the above transcendental structure of union the following important steps constitute the essence of Kant's philosophy;

1st—Transcendental Argument
2nd—Copernican Revolution
3rd—Transcendental Method
4th—The Notion of Critique.

They all form a unity and the aim of this unity is to guarantee the a priori knowledge of the world and to make possible the critical nature of philosophy.

The Sceptic maintains that the world of material objects is a matter of contingent fact and challenges us to show how we know it. According to him any justification of our belief will have to come from within experience, therefore no adequate justification can ever be given. In order to reply to the challenge of the Sceptic Kant puts forward his *transcendental argument*. The *transcendental arguments* are supposed to demonstrate the impossibility or illegitimacy of this sceptical challange by proving that certain concepts are necessary for thought or experience. This *transcendental argument* must either be deductive or inductive, otherwise it would be a sort of mystical argument and the reply to the sceptics challenge would not be possible.

Let us see the structure of the *transcendental arguments*. The conclusion of a *transcendental argument* must be synthetic a priori.[10] If the conclusion should be synthetic a priori then there is no possibility of *transcendental arguments* being inductive in nature. Because the conclusion of an inductive argument can never be synthetic a priori, it never claims necessity and universality for the reason, "experience does not give strict universality". The only possibility left is that of being a deductive argument. Assuming *transcendental arguments* are deductive in nature, let us see their other constituent premises. If the conclusion of the *transcendental argument* should be synthetic a priori then atleast one of the premises of the syllogism must be synthetic a priori and that should occupy the place of major premise.[11] Then the other premise may either be analytic, or synthetic a posteriori, or synthetic a priori. It cannot be synthetic a posteriori, because experience cannot prove the ground of its own possibility, since the proposition aims at the necessary conditions of experience. It cannot also be synthetic a priori because then sceptics may doubt it, therefore the premise could only be analytic. Now the structure of the *transcendental argument* is as follows:

1. Major premise — synthetic a priori
2. Minor premise — Analytic
3. Conclusion — synthetic a priori

To put the argument in a Kantian way it would be:

1. Human beings have experience of a spatio temporal kind.
2. A, B, C, are necessary conditions of that experience, therefore.
3. A, B, C, obtain.

Symbolic expression would be:

P
P ⊃ Q (Q is a necessary condition of P), therefore
Q

In case of minor premise being synthetic the argument would be,

P
Q ⊃ P (P is a sufficient condition of Q), therefore
P (This commits the fallacy of affirming the consequent).

Let us see whether Kant's reply to the sceptics can be justified or not. Since the major premise is so fundamental the Sceptic cannot question it. Certainly this is not an analytic proposition, nor even a mere generalisation. The minor premise which has been accepted as analytic has atleast two reasons for its support; from a philosophical point of view, the Sceptics would not be able to question it and from a Logical point of view, if that would be synthetic then it would have to be formulated as dealing with sufficient conditions and hence would commit the fallacy of affirming the consequent.

Now the *transcendental argument* becomes formally valid and the reply to the challange of sceptics found to be justified. But its acceptability depends upon the minor premise. Those who have argued that the minor premise aims at a sufficient condition of the experience, which is open to sceptic to doubt, for them the *transcendental argument* in principle is mistaken.[12] On the other hand, those who admit that the minor premise aims at the necessary condition of the experience, which is free from sceptics' doubt for them the *transcendental argument* is acceptable, if we could really establish that the minor premise is analytic. Now whether the minor premise aims at a necessary condition or not, becomes a debatable point. Kant himself in a crucial passage in the *Critique* where he is concerned with the status of the principle of *Synthetic Unity of Apperception* states that although the principle is a necessary condition for all synthetic knowledge yet the principle itself is only analytic. "Although this proposition makes synthetic unity a condition of all thought, it is, as already stated, itself analytic." (B 138).

Hence, the acceptability of *transcendental arguments* depends how Kant successfully shows the minor premise to be analytic.

(vi) Conclusion: Transformation of the Problem

Kant called his critical theory of knowledge the Copernican revolution in philosophy. This means that the mind is the only factor, which is always present in experience. And it is legislative for all objects which appear to the senses and are known in judgments; which means that to make a priori knowledge possible, objects must conform to the *transcendental requirements* of the mind. If this revolution is taken for granted, the *transcendental method* follows. To explain it in more detail, if we regard the complete system of a priori cognition as an edifice, the *Transcendental Doctrine of Elements*, examines the materials and their functions, while the *Transcendental Doctrine of Method* considers the plan of the edifice and determine the formal conditions for a complete system of *pure reason*, (B 735-6). While Kant engaged himself in his *Critique of Pure Reason*, he found dogmatists and sceptics on the way and the scepticism of Hume broke his dogmatic slumber. His awakening from dogmatic slumber is an awakening to the necessity of a new method. Hume has shown that it is not possible to prove philosophical issues by empirical and logical methods. That is why Kant has shown a new method, the *Transcendental Method*, (B 811-12).

This conception of the *transcendental method* germinated in the *notion of Critique* in the mind of Kant. As the Copernican revolution aims at rectifying the ambiguity of the existing pattern of thinking, the *notion of Critique* similarly aims at clarifying our reason and keeping it free from error. The purpose of a *transcendental critique* is not to extend the knowledge further but only to correct that and to supply a touchstone of the value or lack of values of all a priori knowledge, (B 26).

Thus the *Critique* is opining up a world of altogether new ideas; that Kant is undertaking the most ambitious task ever undertaken on behalf of metaphysics. Such a critique is therefore a preparation for the complete system of philosophy of pure-reason which was Kant's primary concern in all of his *Critiques.*

Putting this *notion of Critique* through his *transcendental structure* he disolved the controversy of rationalism and empiricism and paved the way for critical investigation further. To explain this in detail we see that rationalists assume there are a priori principles and they give the knowledge of things of themselves, while empiricists assume that the only knowledge is sensible knowledge and there is no place of a priori principles. Kant rejects both the latter view, that they give the knowledge of things of themselves and within sensible knowledge there is no place of a priori principles. But on the other hand, he accepts both the former views, that there are a priori principles but our knowledge is necessarily sensible knowledge. The conclusion derived by Kant cannot be shown by rationalists with their speculative metaphysical method, nor by empiricists with their physiology of mind. Here Kant decisively established a new meaning of "experience". That is, experience necessarily has certain non-empirical conditions of its possibility. What are those non-empirical conditions and how to know them? Kant's answer would be they are a priori and my interpretation in the light of Kant would be, they are innate in a transcendental sense. To put it otherwise, the Copernican turn changes the very meaning of the term, "innate". One can no longer go back to the old meaning of innateness in order to grasp its meaning. The meaning changed because when the concept "experience" changed, it affects all other corresponding concepts. Naturally connecting issues relating to epistemology as a whole get themselves transformed. As we find in Kant, to study transcendental reality we have to adopt a Transcendental method. But when this method of investigation is adopted, all the crucial concepts connected with "experience" and "knowledge" would appear in a doubt aspect—transcendental and empirical. So also does the concept of "innateness".

If we go back to the history of the doctrine of innate-ideas, we find they have mixed up both the sense of transcendental and empirical therefore they confused themselves. As an evidence we see that Descartes' acceptance of the doctrine was somehow in the transcendental sense but Locke confused that and developed his polemic only considering the empirical aspect (sources of the confusion may probably be in Descartes' own formulation of the doctrine). But after Kant, we see, the doctrine in its transcendental sense aims at the justification of non-empirical conditions of experience, i.e., quid juris, while in empirical sense it aims at, quid facti, i.e., the genetic aspect of the doctrine. Now the doctrine is not to be understood in the sense that ideas (all or some) are innate, that there are innate-ideas from the previous birth, intuition gives us knowledge of things-in-themselves and innate-ideas refer to things outside sense-experience etc. The new meaning would be *a mode of organising or synthesising our experience.* This manner or mode is innate. So understood "innate" is a description of *certain mode oj synthesis rather than the product.* The synthesis referred is not an empirical or psychological but a transcendental synthesis.

REFERENCES

1. The reference to the *Critique o, Pure Reasons* are given, in the conventional way, to the pages of the first and second editions, which we quoted in the margin of Kemp Smith's translation ('A' refers first edition and 'B' refers to Second edition).
   Inmanuel Kant's Critique of Pure Reason, trans. N. K. Smith, Macmillan, London, 1961.
2. In Kant's critical writings we find no less than seven different statements of his refutation of idealism.
   i) In the fourth *Paralogism* of the first edition of the critique.
   ii) In the Section 13 (Anm. ii and iii) of the *Prolegomena;*
   iii) In section 49 of the *Prolegomena;*
   iv) In the second appendix to the *Prolegomena;*
   v) In sections added in the second edition at the Conclusion of the *Aesthetic* (B 69 ff);
   vi) In the "Refutation of Idealism" (B 274-8), in the supplementary section at the end of the section on the *Postulates* (B 291-4), and in the note to the new preface (B xxxix-xl);
   vii) In the "Refutation of Problematic Idealism" given in the *Seven Small papers* which originated in Kant's conversations wiih

Kiesewetter. (Cf. *A Commentry to Kant's 'Critique of Pure Reason'*, N. K. Smith, Macmillan, London, 1930, p. 298).

3. "The consciousness of my own existence is at the same time an immediate consciousness of the existence of other things outside me". (B 276).
4. A 84/B 117.
5. In the *Critique of Pure Reason*, thé physiology of understanding occurs twice.
   i) In the preface to the lst edition—A IX.
   ii) A 87.
6. Penelhum and MacIntosh, ed., *The First Critique*, Wadsworth Publishing Company, 1969, pp. 4-17.
7. This phrase is liable to be misleading, but it needs to be considered fairly carefully because some of the most important commentators have placed considerable weight on it.
8. See A 80—B 106 for table of categories.
   See A 70—B 95 for the list of forms of judgment.
   The metaphysical deduction derived a list of 12 categories for 12 concepts of Logic by reflecting on the connection between the general work of understanding in reference and its specific work in making judgments about objects.
9. The lst part of the transcendental Deduction (A 84-95/B 116-29) contains various introductory observation, including an explanation", of the notion of "Transcendental Deduction", criteria of Locke and Hume, who attempted to derive categories a posteriori.
   The 2nd part (A 95-130/B 129-69) which contains main argument, was completely re-written for the 2nd edition, though the difference between the two editions are more of emphasis than of basic content.
10. From two stand points at least we can see the conclusion of the *transcendental argument* should be synthetic a priori.
    From the stand point of example:
    The conclusion of the *Transcendental Aesthetic*; that space and time are forms of intuition.
    The conclusion of the *Transcendental Logic*; categories are necessary conditións of knowledge.
    In both cases the conclusions are synthetic a priori, as they are the products of *transcendental arguments*, therefore, the conclusion of *transcendental argument* is also synthetic a priori.
    From a formal point of view: Conclusions of *transcendental arguments* claim to be necessary propositions. In Kant's philosophy we find two kinds of necessity—a—Analytic necessity; and b—synthetic a priori necessity.
    Here the conclusion can never be analytic necessity because its denial never involves self-contradiction, therefore it must be synthetic a priori necessity.

As an evidence to the above argument a reference is necessary (The First Critique—Op. cit., Penelhum and Mac Intosh), "Transcendental arguments", by Barry Stroud, p. 65. Where it is stated that the conclusion of the Transcendental arguments are synthetic a priori. For Kant, proofs that such and such is a necessary condition of thought or experience in general, therefore, have a special feature which is not shared by other proofs that one thing is a necessary condition of another (A 737), and because they have this feature they can answer the "question of justification".

11. The major premise should be synthetic a priori, because its denial never admits of self-contradiction, i.e., the spatio temporal experience can also be denied, but it would not lead to its contradiction. As it is a reply to the sceptics the major premise should be free from any sort of doubt, it cannot be analytic, already shown, therefore, it must be synthetic a priori, and depending upon the content the synthetic a priori, premise here cannot be doubted by the sceptic.
12. Cf., Wilkerson, *Kant's Critique of Pure Reason*, Oxford, 1976, pp. 199-213.

PART II

Towards A Meta-Theory of Innateness

7

Towards a Meta-Theory of Innateness

(i) The Meta-Theory in its Kantian Formulation

In this chapter, taking theoretical implications of the Kantian revolution, into account, I would suggest the form of a meta-theory of innateness and its implications for epistemology. First of all I would concentrate on what is involved in a meta-theory of innateness and how the Kantian revolution in philosophy has radically changed its claims and methods.

The traditional question was 'What is innate ? a factual and not a transcendental question. But the meta-theory is concerned with what is meant by saying that something is innate or to put it in other words, the classical philosophers have always asked and tried to answer questions like, 'God is innate,' 'all or some ideas are innate,' 'genesis of innate ideas', etc., but they have not tried to answer what is meant by innateness itself. This classical formulation refers to first order while the meta-theory refers to a second-order question as pointed out by Analytic Philosophers. Analytic philosophers, particularly Quine[1] clarifying the notion of Carnap,[2] stated that questions of first-order refer to objects while questions of second-order refer to words. Therefore he writes

"Yet we do recognise a shift from talk of objects to talk of words . . . . It is the shift from talk of miles to talk of 'mile! It is what leads from the material (inhaltilch) mode into the formal mode, to invoke an old terminology of Carnap's. It is the shift from talking in certain terms to talking about them. It is precisely the shift that Carnap thinks of as divesting philosophical questions of a deceptive guise and setting them forth in their true colour. But this tenet of Carnap's is the part I do not accept. Semantic ascent, as I speak of it applies anywhere."[3]

Without going into too much of detail regarding the views of Analytic philosophers and their linguistic pre-suppositions, we can see that second-order questions really are concerned with concepts. It is conceptual analysis which has nothing to do with objects. This sort of question is very close to Kant's transcendental question, which refers not to things but to our mode of knowing things. "I entitle *transcendental* all knowledge which is occupied not so much with objects as with the mode of our knowing of objects in so far as this mode of knowledge is to be possible *a priori*. A system of such concepts might be entitled Transcendental philosophy." (A 12/B 26).

Similarly if the ideas of theory and meta-theory is to be fitted into with this model, we can say, theoretical statement are questions of the first-order, while meta-theory refers to questions of the second-order, because it is about the theory itself. To use a Kantian perspective meta-theory deals with questions about the possibility of a theory.

We may use the model of first-order and second-order questions along with the distinction of theory and meta-theory in our present discussion concerning the classical exposition of the doctrine of innate-ideas. Here we see that so far the problem has been discussed at in a substantive level and not in a methodological perspective. Taking the doctrine of innate ideas, when Plato expounded it in its ontological aspect, Medival philosophers in its theological aspect, Renaissance philosophers in its mathematical origin and British empiricists in their psychological tenet, they were all simply treating the doctrine on a substantive level. However in Descartes besides his ontological pre-suppositions, we also see an anticipation of transcendental query emerging while he was pre-occupied with his system building, but his acceptance of factual claims like 'innate ideas form a class of themselves' spoiled the intended purpose. All these philosophers were just grouping around the factual aspect of the doctrine which refer to questions of first-order. Their analyses never intended the methodological and epistemic aspects of the doctrine. They dealt with questions of *actuality* but not with questions of *possibility*. Kant considered this as a primary confusion, therefore in the transcendental argument he changed from the sufficient condition to necessary condition. Kant's primary function was to disengage the doctrine from its substantive level and to discuss it in purely methodological perspective. This disengagement is necessary because of the traditional continuity of the doctrine, Kant did not inherit the tradition of just accepting the doctrine rather he put questions to the very possibility of the doctrine. Therefore very significantly he did not raise and factual question regarding ideas being innate. He started with logical question and transformed the doctrine into a method. The postive contribution of Kant to this revolution is, to show how this method is to be achicved. Since it is not a question of fact, it cannot be established on the basis of old methods. Hence Kant suggested a proper method for the interpretation of the possibility of human knowledge which is free from the dogmatic assumptions of rationalism and sceptical illusions of empiricism. Hence, the doctrine of innate-ideas which was considered to be theory now appeared in the form of a meta-theory which aims at the possibility of theoretical cognition and its procedure answer is the entire transcendental analysis.

Now the obvious question is how Kant developed his transcendental method in order to achieve his intended purpose. To answer this question is to demonstrate the transcendental argument and how he himself understood that. For him, a philosophical thesis cannot be proved either from common sense or by an appeal to experience. They also cannot be proved by logical demonstrations. Hence the method of proving a philosophical proposition must be transcendental.

For Kant, a transcendental argument proposition does not merely give necessary conditions of the conclusion but it determines the only necessary condition for the truth of the conclusion. If 'X' is the necessary condition of 'Y', Kant claims that 'X' is the sole necessary condition of 'Y'. This is clear in the *Aesthetic*, where Kant gives an account of space. For him the only way of explaining spatial experience is that space is a form of pure-intuition or to put it otherwise, we are conscious of it only by pure-intuition. Therefore, the two other alternatives that of Leibniz and Newton are to be ruled out.[4]

Therefore for Kant space is neither a divine substance anchored in God, nor material, one anchored confusedly in monads, but it is only a pure intuition. Thereby Kant means that this is the only possible way of explaining experience. Hence he claims that for any philosophical thesis there can be only one transcendental proof which he possible through the transcendental argument.

The structure of the transcendental argument has already been explained.[5] It was shown there that both the conclusion and major premise of the transcendental argument are *synthetic a priori* and the minor premise must be an *analytic* proposition. Arguments for the interpretation were also developed there. But critics challenged the very validity of the transcendental argument taking the minor premise as the target. Those who deny the validity of the argument take the minor premise as synthetic. But for Kant even the conditions of synthetic knowledge is itself analytic and the example is his principle of the unity of *transcendental apperception.* Although the *transcendental apperception* is a condition of the possibility of synthetic knowledge it is itself analytic, according to him.

> "This principle of the necessary unity of apperception is itself, indeed, an identical, and therefore analytic, proposition; nevertheless it reveals the necessity of a synthesis of the manifold given in intuition, without which the thoroughgoing identity of self-consciousness cannot be thought". (B 136).

Here is an indication of the point that the second premise of the transcendental argument ought to be taken as analytic. Kant has provided a sketch of transcendental argument, that sketch has to be filled up in order to give a definite direction to the possible conditions of human experience.

In the post-Kantian period three possible lines of further development of the transcendental turn can be seen. They add flesh to the transcendental scheme of the Kantian perspective. They are *Phenomenology, Genetic-epistemology* and *Analytic Philosophy.* They all begin their transcendental investigation of a definite explanation for the possibility of experience taking the transcendental argument as their point of departure.

Although these three intellectual traditions of Phenomenology, Genetic-epistemology and Analytic philosophy have their own specific concerns and although they have developed in a complex manner in their attempts to solve such specific issues, yet they all have a certain affinity with the transcendental philosophy of Kant. For our purposes they may be looked upon as both continuing certain lines of investigation suggested by the Kantian philosophical turn and at the same time strengthening and enriching the Kantian position by means of their more rigorous methods of development. These three traditions therefore bear testimony to the continuing relevance of the fundamental principles of critical philosophy. It is not hereby suggested that these post-Kantian schools do not successfully challenge many assumptions and doctrines of Kantian thought but what is more important to note is the continuance of certain of Kantian themes and pre-occupation in spite of such specific criticisms and disagreements. Indeed we may relate these post-Kantian developments to three aspects or features of the original Kantian system of thought. As a kind of general analogy we may think of these three different lines of investigation as concerned with three aspects of the structure of transcendental argument. Of course this is to be taken only as some kind of analogy what is intended is to bring out the affinity between the Kantian and these three post-Kantian styles of thought.

In the reconstruction of the transcendental argument I have suggested that the first premise is some kind of structural description of our experience; such statements as that our experience necessarily has a sensuous aspect, that our sensibility is of the spatio-temporal kind and so on. These descriptions represent the basic structures of our experience. If all such descriptions could be taken together in their systematic interconnection, then we would be having a total picture of the forms of experience as a whole; such a description would not be concerned with empirical contingent details about the content of our experience rather it would be a description of the essential structures of our experience. Cognition of these structures is not mere empirical cognition nor is it merely a deduction from arbitrary assumed definitions but such a cognition of the forms of our experience is concerned with essential structures and such cognition has a remarkable similarly with what the Phenomenologist call as "eidetic-cognition". A thorough and rigorous attempt to describe these essential structures would hence presuppose the method of phenomenological description. Kant of course did not carry out such description with methodological rigor but in principle this part of his transcendental philosophy seems to call for the method of phenomenological investigations. In some such manner the phenomenological attempts may be located within the overall structure of Kantian transcendental investigation.

The second premise of a transcendental argument is concerned with the necessary conditions of the possibility of experience. The most supremely general and fundamental condition of possibility in Kant is of course the *Synthetic Unity of Apperception.* It is this which by means of its active synthesis grounds the possibility of experience. The various pure concepts of the understanding are, as it were, continued in its synthetic act, from this point of view the transcendental synthesis stands for the general cognitive capacity of the mind. This cognitive capacity is not merely an empirical fact or datum for it is this which lies behind all empirical facts and cognitions. This capacity is therefore in some sense an a priori capacity of the mind which makes experience and awareness of experience possible, in other wards, in this part of his investigations Kant seems to be laying the foundation for a cognitive structural psychology which would account for the basic constitution of cognition as a result of an activity on the part of the subject. Such a cognitive psychology we have fully worked out in the theoretical and empirical investigations of Paiget. Hence, this aspect of the Kantian position may be taken as finding its fulfilment in the Genetic-epistemology of Piaget.

Thirdly, the entire transcendental investigation of Kant emphasises the crucial fact that philosophical claims can be validated not by empirical or merely logical methods; philosophical propositions being synthetic a priori claims require a unique mode of investigation which could settle their validity. Such a mode of investigation Kant calls transcendental and although the whole of the critical philosophy is in one sense a tremendous application of the transcendental method, yet seldom does he explicitly describe the structure of the method itself, he uses the method without giving us a theory of the method. The work of the Analytic philosophers makes a useful contribution here, for they have been most seriously concerned with problems of philosophical method. Starting from Moritz Schlick's ideas about the turning points in philosophy to J. L. Austin and P. F. Strawson, we have a very long and rich debate on philosophical methodology although the terminology used by Analytic philosophers is very different from that of Kant and although they are highly critical of some of the doctrines of Kant yet there seems to be a fundamental similarity between the method of conceptual analysis and the transcendental method. This similarity is seen in different way in each one of the Analytical philosophers I shall be referring to, namely, Moritz, Schlick, Wittgenstein, Austin and Strawson.

From this point of view therefore we may think of the whole movement of Analytic philosophy in our time as a stream fed by Kantian waters. However, this is only one side of the picture for unlike a river and the streams which branch off from it, here the later developments actually enrich and strengthen the parent tradition. If we look at the achievements of Kant from these three post-Kantian perspectives we actually can have a much clearer and more profound grasp of the problems with which he was concerned.

(ii) The Relevance of Phenomenology for The Meta-Theory

In discussing phenomenology, I would restrict myself to Edumund Husserl as the primary representative of the phenomenological movement, as he is being considered the central figure. While dealing with Husserl, my main study would be his "Pure or Transcendental Phenomenology" and how that serves the further requirements of the transcendental investigation of Kant. I would consider the phenomenological movement and particularly "Transcendental phenomenology" as a natural continuation of the transcendental investigation of Kant for the following reasons: It provided the technique of carrying out such an investigation and by providing such a technique it also clarifies the nature of philosophical thinking itself. Both were present in Kant but were implicit. As Husserl conceives of criticism as one of the disciplines of philosophy, phenomenological philosophy is most accurately conceived as criticism. Similarly Kant's *Critique of Pure Reason was* conceived of as a total transformation of philosophical enquiry into transcendental enquiry propounding with rigorous effort to establish the conditions for the very possibility of human experience. The attempt to achieve an alternative method in philosophical enquiry seems very much conspicuous in both and certainly Husserl's phenomenology shares its methodological perspective with Kant even at a considerable later period of Husserl's development.

In the first *Critique*, Kant emphasizes the fundamental place of inner time, the synthetic character of the understanding, the necessity of transcendental ego, the importance for knowledge of sensory perception and other notions, which seem part of the phenomenological investigation. Even Husserl's anti-metaphysical leanings seem unquestionably similar, to Kant's attitude towards dogmatic metaphysical speculations. Gurwitsch, therefore, says, "in the history of modern thought between Kant and Husserl, one does not find a theoretician of subjectivity who is of comparable depth."[6]

When Kant was aroused from his dogmatic slumber, he found that highly significant methodologicai move by means of his Copernican revolution, termed as the "Transcendental-turn". This "new method" proposes that objects must conform to our concept and the conformation would be sought with the determination of whether, by what right and under what conditions these concepts are legitimately applied to objects. This 'turn' to consciousness with its specific methodological content gives the basic sense to the notion of "transcendental". This turn is a methodological move and his *Critique of Pure Reason* is the treatise, which deals with, not of whether there is a priori knowledge, but of how such knowledge is at all possible. The consequence of the transcendental turn is an enquiry into the conditions of possibilities of experience and of knowledge of phenomena, which yields the concrete picture of consciousness as understanding and pure reason. The attempt of Kant regarding the disection of faculty of the understanding itself, which has been conceived by him as the proper task of the transcendental philosophy, has set out upon a fundamentally phenomenological explication. By means of this transcendental turn, Kant claimed to have discovered the essence of consciousness, both as understanding and as reason. Kant's transcendental critique explicates the inherent claims of consciousness, makes it as the focus of enquiry, which attempts to isolate the essentials of human experience and knowledge and to display their inter-relationship. Similarly Husserl characterised his own enterprise as, "a method by which I want to establish, against mysticism and irrationalism a kind of super-rationalism which transcends the old rationalism as inadequate and yet vindicates its inmost objectives."[7] In all these respects Kant's notion of 'critique' coincides with phenomenological "criticism". Hence, Husserl's statement that Kant was, the first to perceive the sense of phenomenology is clearly correct, in spite of their other differences.[8]

As Kant was impelled to establish the transcendental method aroused from his dogmatic slumber in order to justify necessary truths, Husserl similarly conceived of his transcendental phenomenology, hence in both cases the transcendental turn appeared as the only justification of necessary truth. To exhibit the point in more detail, we find that phenomenology has been referred to as both a 'rationalism' and 'radical empiricism'. Husserl's philosophy is rationalistic in that he believes there are a priori principles or "truths of reason"; but he does not agree with traditionat rationalists that there is a faculty of special power of reason that would identify these truths. Rather, these a priori truths are to be located and defended in terms of a special sort of 'seeing and in this sense Husserl claims to be a sort of empiricist. But his empiricism is not the traditional empiricism of Locke, Berkeley, Hume and Mill. He maintains what they would never allow, that is, that there are necessary truths which can be established through intuition. The fundamental doctrine of Husserl's phenomenology can be summarised in the phrase, "intuition of essence". With rationalists, he maintains that we can and do have knowledge which is neither empirical nor trivial; with the empiricists, he maintains that all knowledge comes from intuition. But contrary to both the traditional movements, he insists that intuition itself gives us necessary truth. And as Kant made an elegant list of the fundamental a priori principles basic to the very nature of human consciousness, similarly Husserl's phenomenology is the investigation of the nature of human consciousness with a view towards disclosing certain special intuitions that yield necessary truths. These special intuitions are called 'eidetic" or "essential" and are to be distinguished from the traditional notion of "experience", which is limited to what Husserl calls factual or empirical intuition. His interest in empirical intuition is not an interest in the empirical contents of these intuitions but rather in their essential forms. Hence, it would be very much natural to conclude that both Kant and Husserl are similar, particular in their search for a priori foundations of all experience and knowledge. But the 'intuition' which seems to be the decisive factor in the foundation of the necessary truth for Husserl appears to be controversial, if Kant's notion of 'intuition' is to be taken into account. For Kant 'intuition' does not play such a fundamental role, except in the case of 'pure intuition'. So at one level what Husserl seems to be doing is to extend the scope of intuition, not merely about space and time but about any essential structure, that is any essence. This is partly due to the fact that for Kant the only mode of 'intuition' is sensuous intuition, that is why the categories of the understanding for him are not matters of intuition. There would be another difference regarding 'intuition' between Kant and Husserl. Kant speaks of synthesis proper because he wishes to emphasize the activity involved in thought, whereas Husserl's 'intuition' seems to emphasize the receptivity. This emphasis on receptivity brings Husserl nearer to empiricists than to Kant.

However, in spite of the above differences, the function of the notion 'intuition' for both seems to be basically the same. Husserlian 'intuition' is not something sensuous like that of the empiricists, so far one can say that Husserl in intuition presupposes some activity, which we may call 'synthesis' in Kant, but they are identical, Kantian synthesis may be regarded as the basis upon which the phenomenological 'intuition' can take place. Thus it can be said that in Kant's notion of 'synthesis' and Husserl's thesis of 'intuition' there is onty the difference of terminology, but functionally they address the same problem.

Thus in investigating the nature of human consciousness, phenomenology becomes a first philosophy, it studies essential structures of act and contents of consciousness, a study based not on mere empirical generalizations but on the intuitive grasping of the essence of phenomena. Husserl undertook to examine his entire programme of philosophy and to reformulate it in terms of a new critique of reason, for which phenomenology provided the foundation. To Husserl, therefore, Kant was the protagonists of the critique of reason, only that his own critique was to be even more radical than Kant's critique, because is not only makes metaphysics a rigorous science but includes all philosophy.

Since the publication of this *Ideen*, 'Pure Phenomenology', "the science of the essential structure of pure consciousness", also goes alongwith the name of transcendental phenomenology. The title "transcendental" for which Husserl developed a linking certainly indicated his increasing sympathy with Kant. Hence the claim that Husserl's transcendental investigation is an attempt to further the clarification of Kant may be justified. Because Kant's 'Copernican-turn' which executed the transcendental turn of modern philosophy, is actualised only in Husserlian phenomenology. In view of all the above points, I consider Husserlian transcendental phenomenology as a natural off spring of Kant's transcendental investigation, in order to exhibit, in more detail, the possible conditions of human experience.

Before dealing with Husserl's transcendental phenomenology and Kant's impact on it, it would be necessary to look at the alternative attempts to provide the 'foundations' of knowledge that Husserl rejected like Kant.

Psychologism, is a species of a general philosophical approach called naturalism. According to naturalist, all concepts are abstractions from experience and all knowledge of the world is empirical knowledge; the only necessary truths are trivial and conventional truths. According to psychologists, all non-trivail but apparently 'necessary' truths are not necessary at all, but merely well-confirmed psychological truths. The naturalist insists that a priori principles either are abstract and very general empirical truths or subtle linguistic or logical conventions. Modern empiricists tend to push most of the problematic a priori principles into the class of convention and linguistic truths.

Husserl in his earliest works tended to defend most of these a priori principles as well confirmed empirical generalisations. But subsequently he was impressed by Frege's critique,[9] which changed the entire direction of his philosophy and he tried to understand how a priori principles could be possible. Husserl's rejection of these two alternatives marked his most important deviation from the linguistic direction of philosophy influenced by Frege. After that Husserl rejected 'linguisticism' and 'formalism' along with psychologism, and as an alternative he suggested a thesis reminiscent of scholastic philosophy. He came up with the suggestion that the very structure of human consciousness and a peculiar class of objects called essence, which are not to be discovered in a study of psychology or in a study of syntax and semantics, makes necessary truth true. And this discovery of essences demanded a new and special discipline which is called, phenomenology. This trend of thought was very much there in Kant, in his distinction of "quid facti" and "quid juris", which asserted the inadequacy of the psychological method for the solution of philosophical problems. Nevertheless Kant was criticised for failing to achieve a 'pure' theory of knowledge free from all naturalistic elements. But Husserl undertook to achieve the same, in his own way, by means of the phenomenological method.

Thus for Husserl the target of his phenomenology centre around the concept, "Consciousness" and its phenomenological analysis. The traditional philosophical analysis of "consciousness" has often either fallen into a treatment of consciousness as some mysterious and autonomous realm or substance (Descartes aad British Empiricists) or it has come to deny consciousness altogether and simply talk in a third person if not in behaviourist manner. Husserl criticises empiricists for their "naturalisation" of consciousness and Descartes for his careless phenomenological description, that is a failure to look at what consciousness is really like. In order to explain his own views, regarding 'consciousness' he stated that "consciousness is intentional", the terminology he borrowed from his teacher Brentano. The thesis that consciousness is intentional requires that we distinguish between the act of consciousness and the intentional object of consciousness. Intentional acts are of many kind, loving, thinking, feeling, imagining, perceiving, calculating, asserting, doubting. There is a correlation between act and objects; every act takes at least one object; every object is the object of at least one possible act.

For Husserl, in the traditional view misunderstanding of "phenomenon" arises since they admitted that 'experience' is equivocal between the intentional act, i.e., the experiencing, and the intentional object, i.e., the experienced. But he distinguished the two and stated further that so far as the phenomenon is an intentional object, is not correct to say that it is simply an intuition, nor is it correct to say that is simply an object. Rather, for him, the phenomenon is an *object as intuited.* The phenemenology here after appeared distinctly as the investigation of two complementary issues, one is the investigation of the conscious act and the other is the investigation of the intentional object. However the former leads to existential phenomenology and the latter would be subject of my discussion, since it leads to the central topic of Hurssel's phenomenological reduction.

Pnenomenological Reduction

Phenomenonological reduction or *epoche* (literally, *abstention*), was considered by Husserl to be his greatest 'discovery', because it brings us to a crucial point in his "pure or transcendental phenomenology" and at the same time in the history of phenomenological movement.

The purpose of reduction is to guarantee the "purity" of the description and to enable in the discovery of the essence that are essential to Husserl's analysis of necessary truth. The reduction assures us that the object described by phenomenology would be the phenomenon, or only the intentional object of experience as already shown. There by the reduction compels us to look at what we simply see, without the presupposition of any interpretation imposed upon it. Consequently, phenomenological reduction does not deny any scientific facts, it only suspends them so that the investigation can be undertaken only with what we see.

Reduction guarantees the purity of the description by forbiding us to describe "natural" objects. To put it otherwise, reduction of *epoche* enables us to describe consciousness and its contents rather than the world and its objects.

Phenomenological reduction also guarantees the seeing of essences and not just individuals. The purpose of this reduction is to reduce descriptions to descriptions of essences, that is to focus attention on the meaning of phenomena rather than on the various peculiarities of particular experience.

Finally, the reduction is intended to eliminate from philosophical investigation a number of puzzles, particularly regarding the problem of existence. Phenomenological reduction never questions whether something exists or not and is real or not. Because it describes only the essence, existence is irrelevant. It is not that phenomenologist is not interested in the analysis of what it is for a material object to be but the central function of reduction, according to Husserl, is to "bracket out existence" for the purpose of phenomenology to abstain from asking irrelevant questions.

In the *Ideen,*[10] the implication seems to be that what is transcendental about phenomenology is that it suspends all transcendent claims, that is assertions about reality other than that of consciousness. The fullest discussion of the term occurs in Husserl's last publication the "Crisis of the European Science and Transcendental Phenomenology". Here he wants to assign it a wider meaning in line with the Cartesian approach, according to which a transcendental philosophy "reaches back, (i.e., literally, "asks back for") to the ultimate source of all knowledge,"[11] with the implication that this source is to be found in the ego. The phenomenological reduction makes its appearance when Husserl enters upon the "fundamental meditation" of phenomenology, which is to yield pure phenomena, and which cannot be attained in the "naive" or "natural" attitude. It is at this point that Husserl turns to Descartes. But at the same time, he makes it clear that his own reduction is not to be interpreted as a Cartesian doubt, which denies, experimentally or temporally, the existence of the things reduced. Even the term *epoche* does not mean a form of universal doubt but it only demands, what is it for one to believe in his own existence. To put it otherwise the primary function of all reduction, for Husserl, is to make us aware of what is indubitably given.

Husserl distinguished two stages of this phenomenological reduction. *Eidetic reduction* is the reduction to the essence, and it is a step on the way to the purified phenomena, while the function of *phenomenological reduction proper* is to free the phenomena from all trans-phenomental elements, from all beliefs in transphenomenal existence and leave us with what is indubitably or absolutely given.

To find out the element of transcendentalism here, let us see how Kant conceived of his transcendentalism and its presence in Husserl's phenomenology. Kant, writes, "I entitle *transcendental* all knowledge which is occupied not so much with objects as with mode of our knowledge of objects in to far as this mode of knowledge is to be possible a priori."[12] The specific claim of Kant here is to attend to our experiencing of the objecs, rather than to the object directly, which clearly resembles the Husserlian thesis of *epoche.* The transcendental investigation of Husserl calls for suspension of belief of existence and non-existence in order to achieve this transcendental cognition and *epoches* is instrumental to that.

Husserl describes *epoche'* in negative terms as the suspension of existential beliefs but in his later writings he indicates positively the direction towards which the reduction is headed. *Epoche*, positively, describes modes of awareness of objects but not the object itself. This mode of awareness is not a psychological, empirical or a mental state. It is an a priori awareness, which is evident from transcendental investigation of both Kant and Husserl. The essence of phenomenology corresponds to this awareness of objects. And in order to experience the awareness a certain special intuition is necessary, which is not possible by empirical experience, but by a transcendental experience. As phenomenology is the study of the essential structures of the consciousness comprising its ego, subject, its acts and its contents, it is not limited to psychological phenomena, rather it is carried out with complete suspension of existential belief. Hence the subject of such an investigation would never be an empirical self but a transcendental self. The experien e of such a transcendental self would be an absolute experience, absolute in the sense that no further question behind it is possible. Therefore this reduction is not merely a moving away from the natural world, but a moving towards something and that is none other than "Transcendental subjectivity".

(iii) The Relevance of Genetic-Epistemology for the Meta-Theory

As for Kant neither rationalism nor empiricism can explain the possibility of human experience, similarly here in Piaget neither structure without genesis (counterpart of Rationalism) nor genesis without structure (counter-part of Empiricism) can give an explanation of the possibility of human experience. Therefore the developmental psychology of Piaget would be of much value while explaining the transcendental structure of Kant. If Kant's transcendental argument is to be considered as an explanation of possibility of a meta-theory concerning human experience then a compatible psychology would be a Piagetian developmental psychology,[13] because both thinkers started their investigation of the possibility of human experience from the notion of *Schema*, having their interpretation. The synthesis of human experience which has already been introduced from the Kantian perspective would be cleared up after description of Piagetian *Schematic operations* which attempted an explanation of human thinking. The notion of sehema occupies a very prominent place, because the very concept of experience presupposes the operation of schemas. They play the role of active synthesis and thereby make human experience possible. Hence, Piaget unlike Locke, does not accept a *tabula rasa* theory of the mind,[14] rather for him intellectual operations play an important role in formation of concept, although they are tied up with behavioural activities. Hence my concern would be to explain the operations of Piaget's notion of schema with other corollary functions and to see how he has explained the structural conditions of human experience.[15]

An important feature of Piaget's system is the study of structures of developing intelligence which is opposed to its *function* and *content*. Content refers to raw and uninterpreted behavioral data while function refers to those characteristics of intelligent activity, which hold true for all ages and which virtually define the very essence of intelligent behaviour. According to Piaget, intelligent activity is always an active, organised process of *assimiliating* the new to the old and of *accommodating* the old to the new. *Intellectual content* would vary from age to age in the ontogenetic level, while the *functional properties* of the *adaptational* process remain the same. Besides function and content, Piaget assumes the existence of *cognitive strucrures*. The structure like content and unlike function, undergoes change with age. They are organisational properties of intelligence and are mediators between the *invariant-functions* on the one hand and *variegated behavioural contents* on the other hand and these developmental changes constitute the major objects of study for Piaget.

Piaget, in considerable detail described intellectual functioning in order to give an explanation of human experience. For him, while we inherit the mode of intellectual functioning, we do not inherit the cognitive structures as such, they come into being only in the course of development. He further held that what we do inherit is a *modus operandi* a specific manner in which we establish relationships with environment. The mode of functioning generates cognitive structures in the course of intellectual functioning and constitutes our biological heritage which remains essentially constant through out life. It is because of this constancy of functioning in the face of changing structure, its fundamental properties are referred to as *functional invariants*, which constitute the core of intellectual functioning; in Piaget's word it would be the "ipse intellectus".[16] Those defining attributes which are said to be invariant over the whole developmental span are principally known as *organisation* and *adaptation*. Adaptation comprises two other related but conceptually distinct sub-properties, called *assimilation* and *accommodation*. Adaptation means adaptation to the environment. It occurs when ever a given organism environment inter-change has the effect of modifying the organism in such a way that further interchange favourable to its preservation are enhanced. This adaptation admits of two above conceptually distinguishable components. Although assimilation and accommodation are distinguished conceptually, they are indissociable in the adaptional act. And adaption through its twin components expresses the dynamic outer aspect of biological functioning. Piaget explained that intellectual functioning in its dynamic aspect is characterised by the invarient process of assimilation and accommodation. And an act of intelligence in which assimilation and accommodation are in balance or in equilibrium constitutes and intellectual adaption. Both adaptation and organisation are closely linked, since adaptation pre-supposes and underlying coherence on the one hand, and organisations are created through adaptions on the other hand.

This explanation of intellectual functioning becomes clearer when we take Piaget's notion of schema into consideration. The idea occupies a prominent place in his account of cognitive development, especially during infancy. A schema is a cognitive structure which has reference to a class of similar action sequences, these sequences of necessity being strongly bounded totalities in which the constituent behavioural elements are tightly interrelated. Schemas are labelled by the behaviour sequences to which they refer. Thus while discussing sensory-motor development, Piaget speaks of, the *schema of sucking*, *the schema of sight* and so on, similarly in the middle childhood a schema of *intuitive-qualitative correspondence*, by which one knows whether or not two sets of elements are numerically equivalent. And adolescents possess a number of operational schemas. It would not be accurate to speak that schemas only names by their referent action sequence, they do have more role to play. Schemas come in all sizes and shapes. However they all possess one general characteristic, that is the constituent behaviour sequence is an organised unity. It from the functional invariant angle the schema is to be studied, it is seen that a schema being a cognitive structure, it is fluid form to which actions and objects are assimilated during cognitive functioning. And again schemas being structures they are both created and modified by intellectual functioning. Here a comparison between Kantian and Piagetian schema is necessary. For Kant the constitution of a priori forms do not undergo change whereas schema of Piaget do change. But the methodology of both remains the same, i.e., concept of experience pre-supposes the functioning of certain elements which are not deriavable from sense-content. These are nothing but non-empirical conditions of human experience.

If the operation of schema is to be studied in its dynamic aspect, it would be known how because of schemata, mental assimilation is possible. According to Piaget, one of the most important characteristics of an assimilatory schema is its tendency towards repeated application. In fact, only behaviour patterns which recur again and again in the course of cognitive functioning are conceptualised in terms of schemes. Piaget refers to this repetition as *reproductive and functional assimilation.* Once schemas are constituted they apply themselves again and again to assimilate aspects of the enivronment. In the course of this repeated exercise, individual schemas get transformed in several ways, this sort of functioning not only creates structures but changes them continually. First of all, schemas are forever extending their field of application in order to assimilate new and different objects. This is according to Piaget, *generalising assimilation.* A second important change which schemas undergo that of *internal differentiation,* because of this recognition of certain objects within an initially undifferentiated schema becomes possible, which he regards as *recognitory assimilation.* And the union of these three basic functional and developmental characteristics of all assimilatory schemas, *repetition, generalisation* and *differentiation—recognition,* essentially constitute intellectual functioning. Precisely speaking, the operation of schema during the cognitive development can be explained as follows. Repetition consolidates and stabilizes the schema besides providing the necessary conditions for change. Generalisation enlarges it by extending its domain of application. And differentiation has the consequence of dividing the original schema into several new schemas, each with a discriminating focus on reality. But instead of undergoing individual changes of this kind, it also forms inter-relationships with other schemas. For example, two schemas may undergo separate developments up to a point and then unite to form a single, supra-ordinate schema, which Piaget calls *reciprocal-assimilation,* i.e., each schema assimilates the other.

Now it is found that assimilation and accomodation constitute the most fundamental ingrediants of intellectual functioning. Both functions are present in every intellectual act of whatever type and developmental level. Hence their co-occurrence may said to be strictly invariant but on the other hand their relationship is no constant. Rather their relationship changes completely within and between developmetal changes. Because the functional invariants themselves constitute the core of intelligence in Piaget's system, therefore alternations in the relationship between them must necessarily have important consequences for the kind of intellectual functioning which takes place. Hence an analysis of relationship is as necessary in Piaget's theory as the invariants themselves.

The fundamental transformation in the assimilation and accommodation relationship becomes conspicuous during first two years of life. According to Piaget, assimilation and accommodation are both undifferentiated one from the other and yet paradoxically antagonistic or opposed, to each other in their action during this early period of life, because an object and the activity to which the object is assimilated constitute for the young infant a single, indivisible experience. Thus the act of assimilating an object to a schema is hopelessly confused with and undifferentiated from the accommodatory adjustments intrinsic in this act. It is not that the infant fails to account for the object, rather the infant has no way of distinguishing his acts from the reality events which those acts produce or the reality objects upon which they bear. Or to put it in other words, agent and object, ego and outside world are inextricably linked together in every infantile action, and the distinction between assimilation of objects to the self and the accommodation of the self to the objects simply does not exist. This condition, Piaget describes as *pervasive undifferentiation.* The opposition between assimilation and accommodation stems from this very undifferentiatedness, since the infant cannot distinguish his actions from their environmental consequences. Therefore the necessity to make new and difficult accommodations in order to assimilate novel objects to already established schemas is not possible.

If assimilation and accommodation are undifferentiated and opposed in the radical *ego centrism*[17] of the neonate then how to explain the sensory motor development in their growing articulation and complementation. The network of assimilatory schema is so rich that encompassess and interprete the reality products which accommodation presents to it and this richness of schemas provide a guiding framework of meanings which can explicitly direct accommodatory explorations further into the unknown. Therefore schemas not only interpret what accommodation presents, they also provide knowledge of what it would be next.

Thus it is seen that intellectual activity begins with the confusion of experience and of awareness of the self, because of chaotic undifferentiation of assimilation and accommodation. Hence intelligence begins neither with knowledge of the self nor of things as such but with knowledge of their interaction.[18] Therefore the constant working of accommodation and assimilation gives rise during sensory motor development to an increasingly elaborate and complex schematic organisation. And in this way the transition from undifferentiated antagonism to differentiation and balance or equilibrium is normally established.

Piaget attempted to compare and contrast his theory of intelligence, that is the assimilation and accommodation model to other theories in order to give his views on the role of experience in intellectual development.

To *associationism* Piaget reacts taking its interpretation of experience into account. He rejects the notion that the subject is in simple and direct contact with the real external world. Rather his epistemological presuppositions suggest that the subject-object relationship is a subtle and complex affair which itself shows important developmental changes. His fundamental notion of epistemology is that the cognising organism is at all levels a very active agent who constructs his world by assimilating it to schemas while accommodating these schemas to its constraints.

Piaget's theory of intelligence differs from *intellectualism* or *vitalism*, because for him the functions are invariant but not the structures and that is the point of disagreement. To put it otherwise the constant functions in no way can imply constant structures.

Referring to *Gestalt theory*, Piaget points out that there is difference of opinion about the specific composition of intellectual structures rather than about fundamental epistemology. Basically the Piagetian schema is conceived to be more dynamic in the genetic sense, because it is the product of the differentiation, generalisation and integration of earlier schemas, while the Gestaltian schema is static. Piaget inspite of his critical attitude feels closer to Gestalt theory than to associationism and intellectualism.

Piaget, inspite of his differences, is in sympathy with the theory of *Groping* so far as his emphasis on the role of corrective experience in the construction and transformation of schemas are concerned. The Groping hypothesis does not differ substantially from Piaget's own, to the extent that all trials and errors are undertaken for the purpose of accommodation with reality.

To have a synoptic view, Piaget accepts with empiricism, experience as the *sine quo non*, but submits that is a subtle and complex thing, whose utilization depends upon the subjects structural and functional make up. Like intellectualism there is also an intellectual core which persists throughout Piaget's developmental investigation. But this core is on the one hand not symbolised as a force or faculty and on the other hand, comprises the functional invariants of intelligence rather than variable structures, with Gestalt theory, Piaget emphasizes the importance of organized totalities within the subject. The Piagetian schemasis more dynamic and mobile in structure than the Gestalt form. And finally it accepts with the theory of Groping the interpretation that acts originating in the subject gradually established itself with corrections, as a function of their success in coping with objects.

Thus Piaget's theory of intelligence is a synthesis of several epistemological positions. It retains elements of a priorism, especially in its emphasis on constructive activity of the subject and in its belief that the object is unknowable independent of this activity, yet it rejects a prioristic staticity and absolutism in favour of developmental cognitive forms. In the same fashion Piaget selectively includes and excludes views of associatinism, intellectualism, and the theory of Groping in order to have a theoretical framework of his developmental investigations.

The above observations regarding the structural conditions of human experience which has been undertaken by Piaget needs a further comparison with assumptions of Kant in order to see how Piaget's elaborations are extention of Kant's presuppositions.

Both in Kant and Piaget, the intellect is considered to be an active agency which makes experience possible. When Kant introduced the Copernican revolution, he did not reduce reality to the human mind and to its ideas. He also never suggested that the human mind creates things. Rather Kant's assumptions indicate, that we cannot know things unless they are subjected to certain a priori conditions of knowledge on the part of the subject. Kant's claim is that unless this is to be accepted then we cannot explain a priori knowledge which we do possess. Hence, mind must be thought of as active. This activity does not mean the creation of being out of nothing. It means that the mind imposes its own forms of cognition, determined by the structures of human sensibility and understanding. Therefore the 'synthesis' which Kant talks of here is not a construction but it gets verified by the content. As a result, Kant admitted all cognitive contents must be verifiable contents of sense experience. Here we see how in Kant's thinking both the diving force of idealism and the resistance of realism and equally present. Similarly in Piaget's theory, intelligence is always considered to be on active, organised process of assimilating the new to the old and of accommodating the old to the new. He never admits like Kant merely assimilation or accommodation,[19] rather a synthesis in order to explain the possibility of structural conditions of human experience.

In both we find a picture of novel relationships between subject and object. Both admitted that the relationship between subject and object is not a simple given datum but highly complex. The age old confusing relation of subject and object Kant eliminated through his refutation of idealism. When he particularly rejected Problematic Idealism of Descartes, he made it clear that one cannot have awareness of the subject without the object. Therefore the knowledge of object is already pre-supposed in knowledge of the subject, rather, the knowledge of the object constitutes the necessary condition of the knowledge of the subject. Because the object as given to conscious experience is already subjected to those cognitive forms which the human subject imposes by a natural necessity, for its natural structure as knowing subject. Hence the cognitive forms thus determine the possibility of objects. Similarly in Piaget, one should not start with subject but awareness of the self is complementary to the awareness of the object. Therefore for Piaget knowledge of the self and the knowledge of object are dual resultants of the successive differentiation and equilibration of the invariant functions which characterise sensory motor development. As Kant's primary function is to deal with non-empirical conditions of human experience, Piaget's main concern is similar. Kant argued that experience is not something merely given, it is constituted, and this construction is possible only through non-empirical means. And those non-empirical conditions along-with their relative functions constitute the mojor study of Piaget.

The functional invariants which constitute the essence of intellectual functioning in Piaget is also seen as if a glimpse of Kant. When Kant remarked that the purpose of intellect is to so to connect phenomena so that one can read them as experience, he meant that this reading something is functional invariant. He claimed further this as universal function of the intellect, thus dimly anticipating Piaget's theory of functional invariant of intelligence.

Despite of these similarities, between Piaget and Kant, yet a fundamental difference emerges when Piaget admits structures as variants while for Kant structure is invariant. They differ in their account of structure, because Piaget takes structure at the sensory-motor level while Kant takes it on the cognitive or symbolic level.[20]

In Piaget there is continuation of analysis of cognition and biology unlike in Kant. For Piaget intellectual functioning is a special form of biological activity or to put it in other words, his model of cognitive functioning is in application of the biological order. While for Kant the intellectual functioning is confined with the transcendental subject. Therefore the subject of Piaget is an individual cognizing subject unlike the transcendental subject of Kant.[21] However, the methodology adopted by both remains the same, i.e. explanation of non-empirical conditions responsible for the possibility of human experience.

(iv) The Relevance of Analytic Philosophy for the Meta-Theory

If the Kantian background is to be accepted as a foundation of the meta-theory suggested, then the obvious question arises regarding its further requirements. The Transcendental method which comes out as the primary concern of the revolutionary enterprise of Kant gives rise to further questions regarding its method of explanation, medium of expression and the results of such an investigation. My concern here would be to locate its method, medium, and the result, in terms of analytic philosophy and to show how some linguistic philosophers have successfully established the same; to this extent, they may be considered as continuing the Kantian tradition. While doing so, I would separately discuss Moritz Schlick, as the pioneer in the turning the point of philosophy by developing the method of philosophical investigation and I shall also show how Wittgenstein developed that further, and I shall finally consider how J. L. Austin, claimed ordinary language as the medium of expression. Strawson's idea of a descriptive metaphysics also would find a place in this scheme as representing the results of such an investigation.

Schlick's efforts at establishing a proper method in philosophy within the anarchy of opinions,[22] resembles Kant, because both visualized the same state of anarchy in philosophy. Before Kant, particularly in Descartes, the philosophical and mathematical method were employed together, but he distinguished both and held that the mathematical method can do nothing but harm[23] in philosophical investigation. In order to set philosophy upon the sure path of a science, he distinguished categorically questions of fact (quid facti), from questions of justification (quid juris) and claimed that philosophical problems are not factual problems; they are, however, problems of justification. This was the crucial turn, that he took in order to challenge sceptics and thereby made possibly the progress of philosophical pursuit. Hence to carryout his programme, he introduced a new kind of philosophy called 'Transcendental or critical', its purpose being to serve as an introduction to metaphysics, to warn the metaphysician against fallacies of method and to set him on the right track. Similarly Schlick around whom the *Vienna Circle* centered, embarked upon a vigorous scrutiny of traditional philosophical problems and pointed out the anarchy of philosophical opinions. Like Kant, his primary concern was also very much critical; he exhibited the confusion that was inherent in the traditional philosophical problems, which contributed to some extent the seemingly premature demise of philosophical pursuit. The important reason for this, he claimed, was the misunderstanding and misinterpretation of the nature of philosophy. Hence he distinguished the method of philosophy from that of science; philosophic method deals with discovery of meaning while method of Science deal with discovery of truth.[24] Pointing out this definite change in philosophical perspective, he further exhibited the question of meaning which he presumed to be the turning point in philosophy.

However, if we bring out the two key concepts, already introduced, i.e., quid facti, quid juris, and questions of fact, questions of meaning, from the context of both Kant and Schlick respectively, we find that philosophy is in search of a method, which is neither empirical or scientific nor logical. For Kant, it is transcendental method and the *Critique of Pure Reason* is the treatise regarding an investigation of the same method. On the other hand, for Schlick, the method of philosophy is conceptual clarification, its sole task is to clarify the meanings of our statements. Clearly, like Kant, Schlick admitted that philosophical problems are questions, not of fact, but of language. Owing to all sorts of grammatical and psychological circumstances, it very easily happens that we fall into a variety of conceptual confusions and unclarities, and thereby into paradoxes, contradictions, torturing ourselves with 'insoluble riddles'. But the philosophical method of 'meaning-clarification' acts as a sort of therapy. For Kant, also the task of philosophy was an inquiry. His *Critique of Pure Reason* and its subject matter was concerned with an inquiry in order to resolve the anarchy which arose out of dogmatism and scepticism. Therefore his new inquiry becomes critical rather than sceptical or dogmatic. The method of that inquiry was transcendental, nothing empirical or merely hypothetical has any place in it either as subject matter or as method of argument. Hence for Kant the proper task of philosophy does not consist in the solution of speculative problems, because such problems transcend human powers. All that philosophy can reasonably attempt is to analyse and define the situations. These resemblances, between Kant and Schlick, viewed properly, showed that at the level of method, both envisaged a turning point in philosophy, that is philosophy does not encompas factual problems as its subject matter, rather it concerns itself with conceptual or meta-questions. This enables us to conceive of an altogether new activity-conception of philosophy, that is as a meaning-clarification. This meaning clarification of propositions cannot be science because there cannot be any set of true propositions about meaning. The reason for this is that in order to arrive at a meaning of a sentence or of a proposition we must go beyond propositions, therefore the pursuit of meaning consequently is nothing but a sort of mental activity. By means of this mental activity the meaning of propositions are to be sought putting its constituent words in its linguistic structure and this sort of conceptual analysis, in turn, would help in the clarification of words used in a proper context without having a perfectly clear meaning. Therefore, for Schlick philosophy is to be defined as the activity of finding meaning.[25] In a similar fashion, Kant also admitted, in his time, that the peculiar character of philosophy is an activity. However, the idea that philosophy is an activity, is an incidental point of similarity, since for Kant, the activity conception of philosophy has nothing very much to do with methodology but nevertheless, it exhibits the continuity and impact of Kantian thought on Schlick and more particularly on Wittgenstein. Hence the Copernican revolution of Kant and the turning point of methodological perspective of philosophy, of Schlick, inspite of their own theoretical implications, definitely intend the same spirit of philosophizing, further its importance was strongly felt later by Wittgenstein.

In introduction to his Logic,[26] Kant explains his conception of philosophy, where he distinguishes Scholastic philosophy from that of Cosmic philosophy, the one appeals to skill, the other to wisdom.

"In the Scholastic signification of the word, philosophy aims only at Skill; in reference to the higher or Cosmic conception, on the contrary, it aims at utility; (p. 14). No one can call himself a philosopher we can not philosophize. . . . It is only by practice and independent use of one's reason that one can learn to philosophize, (p. 16). We must, therefore, for the sake of exercise in independent thought or philosophizing look more to the method of employment of reason than to the propositions themselves, at which we have arrived by its means, (p. 17).

In Wittgenstein, this conception of philosophy gets more emphasis, when he states:

". . . Philosophy is not a body of doctrine but an activity. A philosophic work consists essentially of elucidations. Philosophy does not result in 'philosophical propositions', but rather in the clarification of propositions". (Tractatus 4. III-4. 112).

Wittgenstein's Kantian back ground is sometimes elucidated with two remarks from the *Tractatus*—"All philosophy is a Critique of Language", and "Logic is transcendental".[27] When developed, these two statements suggest that the function once performed by Kant's Transcendental Logic and deduction of categories are now supplied by Wittgenstein's logical analysis of language forms and by a Critique of pure language or Transcendental philosophy of language. This interpretation is useful as a retrospective view of Wittgenstein which relates his work to the present analytic interest in Kant.

Wittgenstein suggests that a critique of language is the positive remedy for the condition in which "most of the propositions and questions of philosophers arise from our failure to understand the logic of our language," (T.4.003). In Kant there is a broadly similar recognition that philosophical disagreements follow a pattern and they can be resolved neither by dogmatism nor by scepticism, but only by a critical, Transcendental Logic.

Similarly, Wittgenstein writes "in philosophy the question, 'what do we actually use this word or this proposition for?' repeatedly leads to valuable insights" (T. 6. 211). The Kantian dialectical reason does supply an analogue for Wittgenstein's conception of the active dissolution of linguistic deceptions, just as there is Kantian hint of philosophical awareness as concerned with a sense of reaching limits of human talk and judgment.

Especially in his later developments, Wittgenstein approximated to the Kantian way of philosophizing. There is a broad analogy between his theme of the bewitching effects of language and the Kantian description of the human mind's natural, inescapable attraction toward transcendental metaphysics and its dialectical illusions.[28]

Particularly, if the transcendental argument is to be taken into account, we find a definite resemblance between Kant and Wittgenstein. What Wittgenstein means by "grammatical" knowledge, called by Kant "Transcendental". Cavell[29] remarked that the two are similar can be seen by comparing the following two passages, the first from Kant, the second from Wittgenstein.

"And here I make a remark which the reader must bear well in mind, as it extends its influence over all that follows. Not every kind of knowledge a priori should be called Transcendental, but that only by which we know that and how—certain representations (intuitions or concepts) can be employed or are possible purely a priori. The term "transcendental", that is to say, signifies such knowledge as concerns the a priori possibility of knowledge or its a priori employment" (Critique of Pure Reason—tr. N.K. Smith, p. 96).

"Our investigation . . . is directed not towards phenomena, but, as one might say, towards the 'possibilities' of phenomena". (Philosophical Investigations & 90).[30]

Thus linguistic philosophy could be regarded an enquiry into the necessary conditions for the possibility of language itself; in a similar fashion Kant, tried to discover necessary conditions for the possibility of experience. Hence for the linguistic movement philosophical problems are problems which may be solved or dissolved either by referring the language or by understanding more about the language we use. Because if we carefully examine the language used by philosophers we would find that it is largely the ambiguities of language, the misuses of language, that are responsible for the difficulties of philosophical questions. In fact a large number of philosophical statements and puzzles, wnen analysed are found to be meaningless. It is thus claimed by the Analytic School, that language alone formed the entire subject matter of philosophy and analysis of language becomes the key to philosophical investigations. As an example we find Logic, mathematics and traditional metaphysics are said to consist entirely or almost entirely a priori propositions. But these so called propositions are puzzling because truth of such propositions cannot be established by an appeal to sense-experience, then the problem arises of how such a proposition can have a non-empirical method of validation and what that method is. It has been suggested that the method of validation consists in simply understanding the proposition either by examining the proposition alone, or by deducing it from other propositions so understood, or by some kind of argument that makes no reference to empirical matters of fact. But it may be asked, "what is it to examine a proposition"? or "what is the non-empirical form of argument in question"? Consequently it has been held that a priori propositions are necessarily true. But how any proposition can be not simply true but necessarily true has seemed to be deeply puzzling. Here the linguistic philosophers explain that a necessary proposition is of such a nature that its truth can be ascertained simply by reference to the use of the words or symbols that occur in its expression, without any further appeal to sense-experience. Another type of linguistic theory asserts the sentences that seem to express a priori propositions really express only linguistic rules or rules of inference, that is, their function is to prescribe how certain words or symbols are to be used. While pre-occupied with this sort of linguistic analysis, it is to be noted that philosophical problems are not about language, they are clearly about philosophical concepts. What is urged here is, however, that these problems spring from language, reveal the confusions as to the uses of language, and are to be solved, or removed by employing language properly. This decisive turning point in philosophy brought an end to the fruitless conflict of systems inherent in the traditional philosophical problems. We are at present in possession of methods which makes every such conflict in principle unnecessary. Now it is clear, how linguistic philosophers, inspite of their different views of interpretation, try to endeavour to formulate a common programme, that is, a search for a method, which would help in the establishment of genuine philosophical propositions by means of conceptual analysis. If we recall the philosophical method employed by Kant we find a close similarity. For Kant, the method of philosophical investigation is different from logical and formal sciences, and also from empirical sciences. Kant calls it transcendental which aims at the mode of knowing objects rather than with the objects, whereas analytic philosophers call it conceptual analysis.[31]

If the method of meta-theory suggested would be the conceptual analysis, then what would be its medium of expression.

Suppose innate elements are considered to be the ground of possible experience, for Kant these are categories or fundamental concepts. What would be the medium of expression of those fundamental concepts. These innate possibilities, cannot simply be considered as introspective contents, because it would lead to a form of psychologism of the type which Locke and Descartes accepted. For Kant also psychological methods are considered to be inadequate for solution of philosophical problems he even completely separated the questions of origin from these which relate to value. This trend of thought in Kant becomes more clear with the rejection of the physiology of mind of Locke. There he made the distinction between questions of fact and questions of justification and argued that factual questions are to be removed from philosophical investigation for a better understanding of philosophy itself. If questions of justification, is to be accepted as the only concerns, then the idea of innate possibilities as introspectable states would never arise, because as a philosophical concept their status would be only empirical.

If the medium of expression of those innate elements are not mental states and dispositions which would be a factual question, then what would be the medium of that kind of clarification? The medium is therefore a medium in which the fundamental conditions are expressed and this is the necessarily ordinary language.[32] Broadly speaking the two groups of linguistic philosophers talk about the world by means of talking about a suitable language. The fundamental concern was relating to the method, on which OLP and ILP agree. Equally and fundamentally they disagree on what is a 'language' and what makes it 'suitable'. However my concern is not to point out the distinctive features of the debate that took place between OLP and ILP, but the outcome of the debate is definitely a clear indication of the solution of philosophical problems by means of language analysis. If the method adopted by both is same, then the question arises as to why 'ordinary language' would be preferred as the medium of expression of the meta-theory, instead of an ideal language. To this my submission would be that the starting point in ordinary language, whose distinctive feature is to begin with common and plain language for communication has got very close similarity with Kant. For Kant the categories are categories of ordinary experience, therefore Kant's metaphysics is considered to be the metaphysics of experience.[33] His explanation of the possible conditions of human experience is not at all an artificial conceptual system, rather the main purpose of the *Critique* is to deduce the principles which describe the general nature of the objects given in experience by showing that they describe "necessary conditions of the possibility of experience." With this theme in mind, I would now like to turn to a discussion of Austin, in order to see, why ordinary language should be the medium of expression of philosophical investigations.

The methodological contacts of Analytic philosophy with Kant get somewhat more specific in the writings of J.L. Austin. He is very critical of the conventional handling of epistemological themes through an obsessive repetition of just a few words, facts and examples treated as standards. His main remedy is to attend more carefully to the distinctions operative in our ordinary forms of speech.

In order to carry out his intended programme he adopts the close investigation of ordinary language as his method, a close examination of the language would be at least a "begin—all" if not an "end—all", which mostly found in his papers "A Plea for Excuses" (*Philosophical Papers*, (PP), pp. 175-204) and "Three ways of Spilling Ink" (pp. 272-287).

Austin's central concern is with ordinary language, the language spoken prior to specialist theorizing, and the language of the 'plain man'. He argued that ordinary language already contains finer and subtler distinctions than is often realised, and if those are explored in preference to artificial language then it may be possible to reach agreement and make some progress in philosophical discussion (cf. *sense and sensibilia*, pp. 3, 63, *PP*., pp. 175ff.).

"Our common stock of words embodies all the distinctions men have found worth drawing and the connections they have found worth making, in the life times of many generations: these surely are likely to be more numerous, more sound, since they have stood up to the long test of the survival of the fittest, and more subtle, at least in all ordinary and reasonably practical matters, than any that you or I are likely to think up in our arm-chairs of an afternoon—the most favoured, alternative method". (*PP*-p. 182).

He continued further to assert that—"In view of the prevalance of the slogan 'ordinary language', and of such names as 'linguistic' or 'analytic' philosophy or 'the analysis of language', one thing needs specially emphasizing to counter misunderstandings. When we examine what we should say when, what words we should use, in what situations, we are looking again not merely at words (or "meanings", whatever they may be) but also at the realities we use the words to talk about; we are using a sharpened awareness of words to sharpen our perception of, though not as the final arbiter of, the phenomena": (*PP*-p. 182).

In the above passages which are central to an understanding of Austin's approach to philosophy, the argument is not merely that we need to examine ordinary language so that we are clear on what we are rejecting if we reject it, it is rather that there is reason for not rejecting it. To put it in other words, the concepts we already operate with, have a claim to superiority for otherwise they would not have survived but would have been replaced by more adequate ones. After consideration of the distinctive guidelines of ordinary language, now it is clear, why it is to be taken as the medium of expression of the metatheory.

Now one more aspect of the methodology remains to be seen, i.e., what would be the result of such an investigation.

P.F. Strawson's "*Bounds of Sense: An Essay on Kant's Critique of Pure Reason*"[34] and "*Individuals: An Essay in Descriptive Metaphysics*,"[35] both define the major conditions for another stage of the analytic movement of Kant in the evolution of Kant's interpretations.

Kant's conception of metaphysics of experience, is concerned with the general conditions of the employment of concepts, of the recognition of the particular contents of experience as having some general character; and he regards these conditions as having at the same time the fundamental conditions of ordinary or empirical self-consciousness, has a close similarly with the Strawsonian distinction between Descriptive and Revisionary metaphysics.[36]. Rather to put it otherwise it is his distinction which permits him to respond, to Kant's careful distinctions among the kinds of metaphysics contextually and thematically.

In defence of Transcendental metaphysics, Strawson stated that the execution of this programme may appear to be doubtful, but if these doubts are proved to be unjustified and a genuine inquiry of this kind is possible, then it fully deserves the title of metaphysics. Its method would be non-empirical, not because, like transcendent metaphysics, it claims to be concerned with a realm of objects inaccessible to experience, but because it is concerned with the conceptual structure which is pre-supposed in all empirical inquiry.

Strawson suggests that there are three primary Kantian meanings of 'metaphysics':

1. There is a legitimate metaphysics of experience, analysing the general conditions of human experience and knowing. This finds its counterpart in Strawson's descriptive metaphysics, which inspects the concepts and methods required for an immanent study of human experience.
2. Transcendent metaphysics, both Kant and Strawson opposed, which would discourse about entities supposed to be beyond our experience.
3. Revisionary metaphysics, is vitiated by a defective model of mind made nature and an unintelligible theory of the mind as a process of thinking nature.

Out of these three, my concern is here with descriptive metaphysics because, the result of the investigation undertaken in the attempt to establish the supposed meta-theory would be the same. Because, if the innate elements considered to be the grounds of possible experience would form a conceptual system, which is pre-supposed in all our knowledge, then descriptive metaphysics would be the only result, because it inspects the concepts and methods required in examining the possible conditions of human experience.

Hence descriptive metaphysics becomes the only factor to explain conceptual system, which is involved in any actual claim for knowledge, whether Scientific or formal. The claims of descriptive metaphysics will have a peculiar necessity about them. They are not necessary in the sense of logic, but they are necessary because they are pre-supposed in all knowledge, that is in our conceptual system. Hence to deny to such propositions would be unintelligible. Even the idea of descriptive metaphysics is liable to be met with scepticism. No sceptic. however critical he may be, can make descriptive metaphysics his target, because he cannot simply talk anything without having a conceptual system. Therefore Strawson writes:

> The point is not that we must accept this conclusion in order to avoid Scepticism, but that we must accept in order to explain the existence of conceptual scheme in terms of which the sceptical problem is stated. But once the conclusion is accepted the sceptical problem does not arise. So with many sceptical problems: their statement involves the pretended acceptance of a conceptual scheme and at the same time the silent repudiation of one of the conditions of it existence.[37]

Hence the peculiar necessity of philosophical proposition is that their denial would be unintelligible but not contradictory (in that case this would be analytic but this is not so). So scepticism is not false but unintelligible. Therefore Descriptive metaphysics is an indespensible part of an explanation of the non-empirical conditions of human experience, which would be in Kantian term a Transcendental necessity.

Now to look back for a brief observation, it is found, that the metatheory, which aims at the explanation of non-empirical conditions of human experience, begins with conceptual analysis as its method, eventually progressed within ordinary language as its medium of expression and finally resulted in a form of metaphysics, which even a sceptic cannot question. This becomes possible, when Schlick brought about a turning point of philosophy, opened an era, where the philosopher is free from all sorts of factual claims, but is accountable to meta-questions, Wittgenstein prepared the way for the enlargement of its scope and Austin strengthened it by showing that there is a Kantian transcendental way of asking about the basis of possibiliiy and relationships, in our sensings of thing and ultimately Strawson enabled Analytic philosophy to take the Kantian dimension of the range of problems which determine the direction of philosophy towards descriptive metaphysics.

(v) Conclusion

Substantially the doctrine of innatism has been reviewed, from Plato and it is found that the doctrine maintains its continuity inspite of its contextual changes. Only in Kant, it is clear that the problem of the doctrine of 'innatism' is not to question the genesis of ideas but to search after the possible conditions of human experience. This way of putting the doctrine naturally removes from it all sorts of factual claims and concentrates attention upon the mode of organising or synthesizing experience itself. Hence this manner or mode of synthesis itself becomes the innate-element which is not an empirical or psychological synthesis, rather it is a Transcendental synthesis. As this cannot be studied by traditional methods available, a method unique in its structure has to be sought after and that is none other than the Transcendental method.

The meta-theory which is eventually suggested to study the structure of this transcendental synthesis would naturally demand from us, an account of the cognitive capacity of the mind, which would enable us to know the descriptions of the fundamental structure of human experience, and the distinctive features of its methodology, etc. As a response to the demands of the transcendental synthesis, I have discussed three possible branches of post-Kantian philosophy, namely, Genetic-epistemology, Husserl's phenomenology and Analytic philosophy. Genetic-epistemology exhibits the cognitive capacity of the mind. Husserl's phenomenology defines, the structures of Transcendentalism in a phenomenological manner in order to exhibit in more detsil the transcendental implications of Kant regarding the mode of human experience. And finally Analytic philosophy describes the distinctive features of the methodology concerned.

Thus the meta-theory suggested to study the possible condition of human experience seem to be well clarified by these three post-Kantian philosophies. Genetic-epistemology, supplies the contents of the meta-theory that refers to 'synthesis', conceptual analysis is employed as the proper method to carryout the investigation involved in the 'synthesis', whose results are similar to the 'Descriptive metaphysics' of Strawson and the Transcendental phenomenology of Husserl. But, if we look back, we would find two pertinent questions may be raised here. One would be concerning the attack on psychologism and the other regarding the possibility of the transcendental subject. I would try to answer both questions taking genetic-epistemology into account and would conclude the discussion with a humble note regarding further task to be undertaken.

The attack on psychologism first initiated by Kant, became more prominent in the later part of Husserl's phenomenology and similarly Analytic philosophers for all practical purposes rejected psychologism. The attack on 'psychologism', particularly in its empirical aspect, being eliminated by Kant from his *Critique of Pure Reason*. Because in strict Kantian doctrine psychology and epistemology cannot meet for psychology is an empirical science dealing with the empirical self as a phenomenon among other phenomena, while epistemology is the science of reason itself, dealing with a priori principles on which the possibility of all phenomena depends. As a result, Kant does not propose an investigation of how man's sensory organs function or of how sensations arise. If it were that it would be part of psychology, namely, the psychology of sensations. If it were that it could verify its results only by recourse to observation and the principles which it reached would be empirical. Therefore in *Transcendental Logic*, Kant does not propose an investigation of how all men always think. If it were that, it would be a part of psychology and could not establish any results a priori. Hence, in *Transcendental Logic*, Kant proposes to investigate, whether there are conditions by which thinking is founded, if men were to attain by their thoughts, a knowledge of things. Therefore Kant argues that both Locke and Hume failed to ascertain whether or how metaphysical knowledge is possible, just because they tried to settle this matter by psychology and hence by an empirical investigation. Similarly in *Transcendental Aesthetic*, Kant proposes not an investigation of how sensations arise, but of the necessary conditions to which our sensations are subject.

To make the point more precise, it was the distinction of formal Logic and pure-logic, which led Kant to eliminate psychology as it has nothing to do with canons of understanding, which was the primary concern of his investigations. Therefore Kant remarked :

> "As pure logic, it has nothing to do with empirical principles, and does not, as has sometimes been supposed, borrow anything from psychology, which therefore has no influence whatever on the canon of the understanding. Pure Logic is a body of demonstrated doctrine, and everything in it must be certain entirely a priori."

Husserl as a humble disciple of Kant, attacked Mill's psychological approach to Logic. Mill, in his, *Examination of Sir William Hamilton's Philosophy*, had written of logic that 'as far as it is a science at all, its theoretic grounds are wholly borrowed from psychology.[38] Husserl objects to this, borrowing an argument from Kant's *Critiqne of Pure Reason*, that psychological laws are no more than inductive generalisations, subject therefore to correction in the light of further experience, whereas logical and mathematical principles are 'necessary', they must be true, and therefore cannot be 'grounded' upon inductively derived premises. With its determination to preserve the necessity of the laws of Logic and of the fundamental mathematical principles, he attempted to construct a 'pure-Logic', entirely free from any empirical or psychological premises. Hence his phenomenology neither adopts the stand point nor employs the method of the natural science, because it is not possible from that stand point to arrive at a pure theory, a theory which would be independent of contingent empirical facts.

Analytic philosophers just like Kant and Husserl emphasized the necessity of a clear distinction between empirical psychological problems and non-empirical logical problems.

It holds that we find the traces of subjectivism in the logical system itself, in the discussion of logical problems, mixed with objective logical components, hence the result is inevitably confusing. Therefore to avoid confusion, Analytic philosophers categorically emphasized that no psychological explanation could be the ground of the necessary truth of judgments or to put it otherwise, experience cannot be the ground of necessary truths.

Regarding the second question, the possibility of a transcendental subject or transcendental ego, we find that it has been accepted by both Kant and Husserl but on the other hand, Strawson was dubious about its status. In the hands of both Kant and Husserl, we have the Transcendental method with rejection of psychologism, which resulted in the postulation of a Transcendental subject, because both ruled out empirical sciences as the subject matter of philosophy. Hence it becomes clear here that only the anti-psychologism of Kant and Husserl impelled them to admit a Transcendental subject! this does not seem to derive from merely the Transcendental method. Therefore if we can overcome anti-psychologism, it would be possible to use the Transcendental method without a transcendental subject. Even the status of the Transcendental subject seems to be peculiar to Strawson, so that he claimed the subject of the Transcendental psychology as "imaginary" in the Kantian model.[39]

Piaget's genetic-epistemology seems to answer to the above two questions. The developmental psychology of Piaget, suggests, that psychology need not be under-stood purely as an empirical science, as it has so often been understood, it has also its cognitive parts which contribute towards a new look in perception.[40]

The cognitive function can be divided into two broad categories according to whether the "figurative', or "operative" aspects of knowledge predominate. The "figurative aspects" bear on its observable configurations while "operative aspects," by contrast bear on the transformation of one state into another and therefore include actions and operations, which both aim at the unobservable. Of these two, in the realm of perception, operative aspects play a much greater part. The importance of operative factors lie in stressing the function of "perceptual categorising". Piaget emphasised this cognitive aspect of psychology and claimed that those who have attacked psychologism also follow the same cognitive structure. Hence the questions of cognitive structure cannot be ruled out from any type of epistemology whatsoever it may be. To examine the possible epistemologies in this context, we find the empiricist tradition, those who have recourse to psychology were content with common sense ideas and with speculative descriptions because of the influence of experimental psychology which prevented them from seeing that experience is always a process of assimilation to existing structures. Epistemologies, even those which are anti-empiricist, raise questions of facts and thus implicitly adopt psychological positions which, however, lack effective verification, even though this is indispensible as far as sound method is concerned. Therefore to conceive of a satisfactory explanation of human experience, a consideration of cognitive structure is essential because relative to the contents of behaviour the schemeta are a priori and it is this which makes experience possible.

This acceptance of psychological elements in explaining the possibility of human experience rules out the postulation of a transcendental subject, because it was the anti-psychologism which was responsible for such acceptance. But in terms of Piaget's cognitive psychology, it is the 'epistemic subject,' which is required to make human experience possible by means of its operational behaviour. For Piaget the very notion of a transcendental subject is nothing but that of an epistemic subject. Therefore, Piaget rightly said in connection with Husserl, "Husserl's fundamental mistake lies in the fact that his transcendental subject is still a subject and that "pureintuition" is still the activity of a subject (in which the "object" or "essence", admittedly enters in, but if there is, intuition there is, nonetheless, a subject): it follows that, "transcendental" or empirical, reference to such an intuition is still psychologism, that is to say, a passage from fact to norm."[41] The very assumption of the epistemic subject, therefore, eliminates the notion of a Transcendental subject, in order to account for transcendental cognition. Hence we would have a transcendental method without pre-supposing a transcendental subject.

In the light of the above position, if we go back to the basic notion of "innateness", that is the synthesizing or organising activity of the mind in making human experience possible, we find that this notion has been well clarified by the triangular contribution of genetic-epistemology, Husserl's phenomenology and Analytic philosophy. The schematic operation which makes mental assimilation possible by means of the assimilation and accommodation mechanism constitutes the most fundamental ingrediant of intellectual functioning. And their synthesis is considered to be the ground of possibility of experience. Those conditions which are involved in this 'synthesis' are considered here as the non-empirical conditions of human experience in the Kantian sense, and those conditions are considered to be essential for whatever type of experience it may be, because the organisation of these conditions are necessary preliminary to all experience. Hence, it is in this sense, i.e. the discription of this mode or synthesis, is considered that we can speak of "innate" and not any product. This synthesis never needs a Transcendental subject for its explanation inspite of its being transcendental, because this transcendental synthesis is within the reach of the epistemic subject. Otherwise, this 'synthesis' is natural but its function is transcendental. Hence, the new understanding of the *innate as synthesis* can be had in the purified form of a transcendental theory without a transcendental subject.[42]

This is certainly a beginning venture in searching for an adequate solution of some problems of the theory of knowledge; the discussion has been mainly concerned with how one should properly formulate and construe these problems. I have been trying to concentrate upon certain essential conceptual, methodological and epistemological preliminaries which must be considered first, before we can state the basic issues in the theory of knowledge properly. Hence, my main concern is not so much with a theory of innate ideas, as with a meta-theory of innateness.

It is evident that a risk has been taken in suggesting the meta-theory, the risk, namely, that epistemological consequences may follow from psychology. If the answer would be positive, the controversial problem, psychologism would be solved. But apart from this many more questions may arise, which I cannot pursue here. But I can atleast submit that in this thesis an attempt is being made to discover an alternative method for epistemology, hence, a risk is inevitable. Therefore, I conclude my reflections with a remark of Wittgenstein :

> "As regards his own work, he said it did not matter whether his results were true or not: what mattered was that 'a method has been found'."[43]

REFERENCES

1. W. V. O. Quine; *Word and Object*, (Massachusetts Institute of Technology Press—1960).
2. Rorty, Edited, Linguistic Turn, ("Empiricism, Semantics, and Ontology", Carnap, University of Chicago Press, 1968).
   The confusion arose in Carnap because for him there was no genuine philosophical questions. He distinguished the questions of first-order and second-order into theoretical and practical questions respectively. For him particularly, the theory of knowledge was not at all a distinct study of some importance. Therefore, for him some questions of epistemology either merged in Logic, that is second-order or some in psychology of first-order. But Quine made it clear that philosophical questions are significant. He, just like Kant identified epistemological questions and categorised them distinctly that they are conceptual questions. When Kant raised his transcendental question regarding the possibility of human experience, he was not doing anything else except a conceptual analysis.
3. Quine—Op. cit., pp. 271-72.
4. For Leibniz on the one hand space was interpreted relationally, on the other hand it was declared to be a mere phenomena, reduciable, to the monads and not ultimately real. Kant discusses the former position in the *Aesthetic*, where he compares the doctrine of Newton and Leibniz (A 39/40) (B 56/57). His objection to the first aspect of the Leibniz's theory is simply that a relational theory makes geometrical propositions a posteriori instead of a priori, the latter status Kant always claims for Euclidean geometry. The argument against the second aspect occurs more explicitly in *Amphiboly*, though there is also an allusion to it in the earlier place, (A 267/B 323/B 331/A 275/B 67).
   Newton, has stated in the *General Scholium to the Principia*, that time and space exist in the virtue of God's filling eternity and immensity. Therefore he writes:
   "(God) endures for ever and is everywhere present; and by existing always and everywhere, he constitutes duration and space."
   Newton's affirmation that space is somehow an aspect of God's

immensity is on the surface irrately rejected by Kant. Referring to the suggestion that 'God is comprised in infinite space all at once', he reacts with the comment that 'words cannot express the extent to which philosophers are befooled by these shadows that flit before the intellect' (Inaugural Dessertation. 85, para 27). Cf. Gerd Buchdahl, *Metaphysics and the Philosophy of Science*, The Classical origins Descartes to Kant, (Basil Blackwell, Oxford, 1969). pp. 574-605.

5. See pp. 193-200. (In This Thesis)
6. "The Kantian and Husserlian conception of Consciousness", Aron Gurwitsch—studies, p. 148 (Cf. Richard M. Zaner, *The Way of Phenomenology*: *Criticism as a philosophical discipline*, Pegasus, New York 1970) p. 97.
7. In a remarkable letter of March 11, 1935, to Lucien Levy-Bruhl (Cf. *The Phenomenological movement*: *A historical Introduction*, Herbert Spiegelberg; Vol. I, p. 84, Martinus Nijhoff, The Hague-1971).
8. In ideas (*Ideas*: *General Introduction to Pure Phenomenology*, translated by W. R. Boyce Gibson (New York: Collier Books, 1962), Husserl explicitly says that it was Kant who first truly perceived the fundamental sense of phenomenology, "although he was not yet able to appropriate it and recognise it as the center from which to work up on his own line a rigorous science of Essential being". (Cf. *The Ways of Phenomenology*, Zaner, p. 98).
9. Husserl enthusiasm for psychologism was utterly destroyed by a review of his book "Philosophy of Arithmatic," by the great mathematician Gottob Frege, who stated that no psychological analysis could explain the necessary character of mathematical judgments. According to Farber, William James also helped Husserl to emancipate himself from 'Psychologism'. The reference is presumably to Jame's chapter on 'Necessary Truth' in the *Principles of Psychology*, where James argues, against Mill and Spencer, that Logic and mathematics have as their subject matter 'ideal and inward relations amongst the objects of our thought'. Husserl also refers to Natorp's criticism of psychologism as expressed in an article on 'The Objectives and Subjective Foundations of Knowledge' (Philosophische Monatshefte, 1887, (Cf., Passmore's, *A Hundred Years of Philosophy*, Penguin Books, 1975). p. 556.
10. Cf., Op. cit., Spiegelberg; p. 126.
11. Cf., Ibid., p. 126.
12. Op. cit., Kemp Smith—A 12.
13. Every distinctive epistemology may be associated with range of compatible psychological theories. The relationship between epistemological theory and associated psychological theories is not one of strict logical derivation, but it may be called a relation of 'affinity'. It is in this sense of affinity that Kant's epistemological analysis and Piaget's genetic psychology may be associated.

14. Cf. Jean Piaget, *Insights and Illusions of Philosophy*, Routledge and Kegan Paul, London, 1972, p. xi.
15. Basically all references of mine here conferred with *The Developmental Psychology of Jean Piaget*, John H. Flavell, D. Van Nostrand Company, Inc. 1963. Part One: The Theory, pp. 15-266.
16. Seems to recall the remark of Leibniz's "nisi ipse intellectus", (except understanding itself). This formulation suggests intellect is an activity but not content. And this is what Piaget clearly says, that the intellect is defined by its function not by its structure. Therefore he remarked that intelligence could not be able to apprehend data without certain functions of coherence and function making relationship, which are common to all intellectual organisation.
17. For Piaget, the ego centrism is the initial undifferentiation and antagonism between the functional invariants. (Cf., Op. cit., Flavel., p. 60).
18. This seems to be corresponding to Kant's main conclusion of his discussion of problematic Idealism.
19. Here assimilation and accommodation of Piaget correspond respectively to idealism and realism.
20. The difference is very much plausible because for both Kant and Piaget there is a fundamental change so far as the beginning of their investigation is concerned. While Kant since beginning rejected the adequacy of psychology to solve the philosophical problems, on the ground of being merely an empirical study, on the other hand, Piaget started his investigation assuming the principles of Psychology, of course a developmental psychology, as the foundation for the study of epistemological problems involved in philosophy.
21. While in some sense some philosophers, especially idealist philosophers have taken the transcendental subject as super individual, a metaphysical subject. It is not necessary to understand it in that idealistic manner. The Transcendental subject may be understood as Kant's way of emphasizing the common structural conditions of all human thinking as such the Transcendental subject is not an entity. His statement that "I think" is to be understood purely as formal unity not as metaphysical entity, suggests this. If this interpretation is accepted the terminology of Transcendental subject need not mislead us.
22. Cf., A. J. Ayer, Edited, *Logical Positivism*, (The Free Press 1959), "The Turning Point in Philosophy", by Moritz Schlick. pp. 53-9.
23. Op. cit., Kemp Smith, A-726/B-754.
24. Cf., Rorty, Edited, *Linguistic Turn*, (University of Chicago Press, 1967), "The Future of Philosophy", Moritz Schlick. pp. 43-53.
25. Cf., Op. cit., Rorty, p. 50.
26. T. K. Abbott, *Kant's Introduction to Logic*, tr. (New York, Philosophical Library, 1963).

27. Wittgenstein, *Tractatus Logico—Philosophicus,* tr- D. P. Pears and B. F. McGuinness, 4.0031, 6. B. For a More thorough comparison, please refer to, *Wittgenstein's Doctrine of the Tyranny of language,* by S. M. Engel (Martinus Nijhoff/The Hague, 1971) pp. 43-73.
28. "Philosophy is a battle against the bewitchment of our intelligence by means of language". (Wittgenstein, *Philosophical Investigations,* tr. G. E. M. Anscombe No. 109, Macmillan, 1968). The confusing effect of language in the service of uncritical metaphysics is prominent in Kant's account. Ordinary text book metaphysics "favoured conceit by venture-some assertions, sophistry by subtle distinctions and adornment, and shallowness, by the ease with which it decided the most difficult problems by means of a little school wisdom, which is only the more seductive, the more it has the choice, on the one hand, of taking something from the language of science and, on the other, from that of popular discourse—thus being everything to everybody but in reality nothing at all". (Kant, *Prologomena to Any Future Metaphysics,* tr. L. W. Beck, Indianpolis: Bobbs. Merril, 1950, p. 132).
29. Wittgenstein: *The Philosophical Investigations,* Edited by George Pittcher, (Garden City, New York: Anchor Books, Doubleday and Co., 1966).
30. For further information reference may be done to the article, Stanley Cavell, Edited by George Pitcher, op. cit.
31. John Dewey—"Kant and philosophic Method", in the *Early Works of John Dewey*, Vol. I: 1882-1888, p. 437.

    Dewey said ninety years ago, about the cardinal role of Kant's method of analytic and experimental reason, still holds good. "It was the suggestion of this method, it was the suggestion of so many means for its execution, it was the actual carrying of it out in so many points that makes Kant's 'philosophy' and the critical philosophy, and his work the crisis, the separating, dividing, turning point of modern philosophy".
32. Pre-occupation with language has been a distinctive feature of twentieth century philosophy. The idea is that language can be made to yield truths about philosophical concepts on solutions to problems answering them. Frege and Russell were first to formulate this idea, and Moore helped to promote with least interest in language as such. The most prominent of this linguistic conception of philosophy, was Wittgenstein. Two different views regarding language appeared corresponding to Wittgenstein's earlier work *Tractatus* and the later work *Philosophical Investigations.* The version which came from Tractatus promoted by logical positivists, turns about the notion of Ideal Language (IL). The premise here is that ordinary language (OL) is somehow deficient or faulty, atleast for philosophical purposes and the clarification and dissolution of problems is to be achieved by constructing a logically perfect language with which to replace it. The other version appeared from

Philosophical Investigations, whose conviction is that "Ordinary language is all right", and that philosophical difficulties, which are linguistic in origin, arise not because our language is faulty, but because philosophers misdescribe it and misconstrue it. To achieve success in philosophy and to solve problems, is to determine how our language is infact used, and thence show where and how philosophers have gone astray. It is this latter version of the linguistic conception of philosophy to which the term (ordinary language philosophy) has been applied. The OLP has been practised by two main philosophical groups. The first comprises those, who were influenced more or less directly by Wittgenstein. They are chiefly Wisdom, Malcolm, Waismann, Anscombe, Lazerowitz etc. The other main group of OLP is that which grew up at Oxford, under the leadership of Ryle and later of Austin. Its most distinguished member after Ryle and Austin, are Strawson, Hart, Hampshire, Hare, Urmson and Warnock; and host of others. Generally presumed that the Oxford philosophers tend to be more interested in the actual details of language than the Wittgensteinians, who tend to restrict themselves to the solution of specific problems, Particularly Austin carried the attitude of disinterested curiosity about the working language further than anybody.

33. Both Paton and Kemp Smith, however, declare that Kant holds that metaphysics is possible as science as a '*metaphysics of experience*'.
    Paton—"a metaphysics of experience . . . so we may suitably describe what Kant calls (in B XVIII) "metaphysics in its first part" Book 1, p. 72 (*Kant's Metaphysics of Experience*, 2 Vols. London, 1936).
    Smith—'Kant's primary interest is in the Metaphysics of Experience' (p. 390), *A Commentary to Kant's 'Critique of Pure Reason'*—(Macmillan, 1930).
34. P. F. Strawson—*Bounds of Sense*: *An Essay on Kant's Critique of Reason*. (Methuen & Co. Ltd., London, 1966).
35. P. F. Strawson—*Individual*: *An Essay in Descriptive Metaphysics*. (Matheun & Co. Ltd., London, 1959).
36. In order to back his sharp dualism between Descriptive and Revisionary metaphysics, P. F. Strawson correlates the former with a stylistic rendering of an invariant core of human categories and the later with an effort to reach new conceptual schemes·
37. Op. cit., *Individual*, p. 106.
38. Cf., John Passmore, *A Hundred Years of Philosophy*, Penguin Books, 1975, p. 186.
39. Op. cit., Strawson, *Bounds of Sense*, p. 32.
40. Regarding the issue of psychologism the contemporary debate between Hamlyn and Toulmin, can very well be acknowledged here, in order to give a definite guide lines to the proposed meta-theory. The central point of the debate is, whether the genetic-epistemology admits of incoherence or a greater coherence can be hoped?

Hamlyn's central concern is that "A theory that rests directly upon both empirical and philosophical consideration must have a degree of incoherence." Admitting this as the major concern, he states that Piaget's term 'genetic-epistemology' to describe his theory of intellectual development in the individual, Hamlyn argues that the term itself is curious one, it does not entirely reveal its meaning and consequently, he (Hamlyn) claims the term to be incoherent. Because the questions regarding genesis of our ideas are questions of psychology, they are not certainly of epistemology and if Piaget would suggest developmental psychology as his theory to explain epistemological assumptions, then certainly, Hamlyn affirms, it is a terminological confusion. Regarding the "forms of understanding", the genuine philosophical question would be about the conditions which are normally necessary if one is to be said to have a certain form of understanding, while questions about the origins of that form of understanding would be psychological. Hamlyn suggests further that our proper task should be to settle the question of status of psychological questions, which Piaget's discoveries never intend. For Hamlyn, Piaget's theory is a blend not only of 'the empirical and conceptual but of the empirical and the philosophical.' Therefore he states the theory to be incoherent. Hence Hamlyn rightly remarked that, "My own opinion is that the mixture of philosophical and empirical issues involves in each case a muddle, that the philosophical and psychological questions which are at stake are different from each other, and that there are no grounds for the belief that philosophical questions can be answered by appeal to empirical evidence or *vice-versa.*" Finally regarding the relevance of genetic-epistemology, he concedes that if at all it has got any relevance for epistemology it is because genetic-epistemology presupposes a traditional epistemological position and not because of its status as a psychological theory.

Toulmin states that Hamlyn may be right in pointing out that Piaget has not taken sufficient care to distinguish explicitly between the conceptual and empirical aspects of his work. But the proper remedy, Toulmin argues, may not be that which Hamlyn prescribes, namely, to separate the philosophical and psychological issues and deal with them independently. He comments that such a separation would be artificial and damaging. Consequently he suggests, we must recognise that in a young science, like developmental psychology, some initial incoherence is unavoidable but greater coherence can be hoped for only if we allow our conceptual insights and our empirical knowledge to cross fertilize in order to have a satisfactory account of the subject. Taking the point of 'incoherence' from Hamlyn, he argues further that it would be acceptable provided Hamlyn would agree that some degree of 'incoherence' has a necessary and creative part to play in the development of sciences. As a result, Toulmin cites examples of physics and mechanics, those who rest directly upon a mixture of empirical and conceptual, or scientific and philosophical considerations. According to Toulmin, his difference with Hamlyn are concerned with question of method rather than of substance. To illustrate this point, Toulmin cites examples of both 'Baconian' and 'Cartesian' over simplifications that Piaget himself condemns and attempts to avoid. And consequently Toulmin admits that those who approach the study of child development from a psychological direction are more prone to the Baconian empiricism, and those who come from philosophical direction are to the risk of Cartesianism. Therefore, Piaget, Toulmin asserts, can be criticised as adopting too empiricistic attitude. But on the other hand, Toulmin asserts, that the mixture of conceptual and empirical consideration, which are unavoidable, needs a philosophical critique of developmental psychology of Piaget's type in order to arrive at a better "theory of cognition" or to put it otherwise at a better "principles of human understanding". Therefore Toulmin admits that in the areas of the discussions of human understanding, the line of separation between empirical issues from conceptual issues or 'scientific' from 'philosophical' is very thin. If at all one wants to distingsuish two groups of issues, Toulmin states, that one cannot succeed in setting them apart from one another. Hence, for Toulmin the central point is while in discussions of intellectual and mental development, one can and should distinguish conceptual issues from empirical issues but they cannot completely separated or dealt with entirely independentally. Therefore he rightly remarked: "In the epistemic field, the traditional issues of philosophical epistemology blend into the most general problems of psychological theory without any sharp dividing line, and are—in actual practice inseparable from them." Cf., Theodore Mischel, ed. *Cognitive Development and Epistemology*, (Academic Press, 1971) pp. 3-60.

41. Jean Piaget, *Insights and Illusions in Philosophy*, Trans. Wolfe Mays, (Routledge and Kegan Paul, London, 1972) p. 104.

42. In Kant reason has a transcendental function in the sense that by means of an application of the forms of sensibility and the categories of understanding it constitutes the objects of experience. This constitutive function presupposes a capacity for categorising, this in turn is based on man's unique capacity for language. At the same time language in its other aspect is certainly a property or capacity of natural beings. Hence, the human subject looked in terms of the capacity for speech and communication may be thought of as a natural subject with a transcendental function.

    "What raises us out of nature is the only thing whose nature we can know; language". Cf. J. Habermas, *Knowledge and Human Interests*, translated by J. Shapiro. (London, 1972) p. 314.

"Ordinary language is the only phenomenon available to us which contains at the same time an empirical and a transcendental moment".

Cf. Wellmer, "Communication and Imancipation", John, O' Neil, edited, *On Critical Theory,* (New York, 1976) p. 245.

43. G. E. Moore, *Philosophical Papers,* (George Allen and Unwin, London, 1959) p. 322.

Appendixes

APPENDIX A

A NOTE ON AGENT INTELLECT

Augustine's epistemology holds that sensible knowledge can never produce certainty. Therefore rational (non-empirical) knowledge is superior to perceptual (empirical knowledge. Here the obvious question arises; 'Is there anything superior to reason ?' Since reason is the man's highest power, if there is any faculty superior to reason, it must be sought outside human nature, that is in God. For Augustine, Aristotelian abstraction from sense-experience is also not acceptable. He also rejects the Platonic notion of previous existence of soul. As he could not find any satisfactory solution within existing theories, he claimed that one must take recourse to God, because God teaches and illumines our mind. He adopted the mataphor as the eye cannot see without the light similarly the soul is blind without an internal light. God is internal light within us who illumines the darkness of our minds. This is known as the Augustinian doctrine of Divine Illumination. Through this light of intellect we see thc eternal truths.

Many thinkers tried to minimize the difference between St. Augustine and St. Thomas Aquinas and to give to Divine illumination a role approximate to that of Active or Agent intellect. Particularly Randall's line of thinking developed in this way, to quote him.

"The functions of the Divine illumination in Augustine and of the Active intellect in Thomas differ, however, because of their different conceptions of the soul and of experience, and the different problems the two men are facing in connection with knowledge. The Thomastic Active intellect "abstracts" intelligible forms from the sense images or phantasmata by which they are brought into the soul from the outside world; it abstracts concepts or universals from particulars, and actualizes them in the mind. But there is no need for the Augustinian Divine illumination to "abstract" anything, for ideas are already in the soul, and are there as universals, not as embeded in particulars. It does not actualize ideas; its function is to make us see their truth, their certainty. Augustine is offering a theory of truth and judgment, not a theory of the formation of concepts—a theory of Logic, not of Psychology. What we see in the Divine light is the truth of our ideas, not their content; from it we gain a standard of judgment; not a source of information. And though men find it by forming within, that standard comes from without—not from the rationality of man, but from the intelligibility of the universe of truth. The mind needs the Divine light to judge what ideas are true, as the will needs the Divine Grace to choose what is good."[1]

This idea of Randall establishes how the role of Divine illumination approximates to that of Agent intellect besides their own way of abstractions. If this is so, the next pertinent question would be, whether the Agent intellect forms a part of the individual soul (mind) or remains outside of it. Aristotle, who introduced the Agent or Active intellect, could not give any satisfactory answer to the relationship of mind to the Active-intelligence. As a result we find the debate has been undertaken by Arabian thinkers, of whom Thomas Aquinas became a strong critic.

To explain in detail; one of the most conspicuous attempts of various Arabian thinkers were to interpret the doctrine of Active and passive intellect. Aristotle's somewhat vague description in the *De Anima* offered an opportunity to them for this. In the Third Book of the *De Anima*, Aristotle had been considering the intellect as though it were a complete unity; then suddenly he tells us:

"Now since in all nature there is a factor that is as matter in the genus, and is potentially all that is in the genus, and something else which is as cause and agent as making everything in it (Thus art is related to its material): so there must be these differences in the soul. There is that intellect, which is such as being able to become everything; and there is that which acts upon everything, as a sort of state, like light; for light too, in a way, makes potential colours actual".

"And this intellect is separable, uncompounded and incapable of being acted on, a thing essentially in act. For the agent is always more excellent than the recipient, and the principle than its material.

"Knowledge in act is the same as the thing itself. But what is potential has temporal priority in the individual; yet this is not true universally, even with respect to time. Mind does not know at one time and not know at another time.

"Only separated, however, is it what it really is. And this alone is immortal and perpetual."

"It does not remember, because it is impossible; the passive intellect is corruptible, and the soul understands nothing apart from this letter."[2]

There is little doubt what Aristotle has in mind in this chapter. He realised that all thinking involves the two moments of the creative activity of the knowing subject and the apprehension of the independent truth of the thing known. On the one side of receptivity, sense receives the sensible forms through the actions of sense-organs and on the other side an element of synthesis is necessary. If either side is ignored, the process of knowledge remains unexplained.

But surprisingly the same chapter of the *De Anima* has been interpreted differently by immediately following thinkers. Four main such interpretations are possible:

1. Active and Passive intellects are only two phases of the one intellect, it may be said that Aristotle never intended to make such a clear cut distinction as some of his commentators have understood. However, such evidence, as we possess, seems to contradict this opinion.
2. Active intellect is impersonal and separate from the individual soul; either it is a world intellect or is identical with the Active intellect of God. This interpretation was adopted by Alexander of Aphrodisias and by the earlier Arbian thinkers.
3. Active intellect forms part of the human soul but is

separate from the body and the sense faculties because it does not make use of a bodily organ. This view was that of Albert the great and St. Thomas Aquinas.

4. In addition, there was the doctrine of Averroes, who not only maintained the unity of the Active intellect but also declared the passive intellect to be one in all men.

The above four possible interpretations can be reduced only to two important alternatives. One would be, that the Active intellect is an intrinsic component part of the human intelligence, the opinion of Thomas Aquinas. The second would be, that Agent intellect is an agent coming into the soul from outside or a separated substance, as has been accepted by almost all Arabian thinkers.

All Arabian philosophers have accepted Agent intellect as the last of the pure intelligences which governs our world and the highest act of man is to become united with Active intellect by means of moral life and philosophic contemplation. Since the Active intellect is separated from man and is unmixed with matter, it must be one, and the idea of number can be applied only to the individuals who participate in it. The human intellect is the subject which receives the form of Active intellect. As the sun by bestowing light, enables the eye to see, so Active intellect illuminates the intelligible idea and enables the human intellect to realize its capacity for knowledge.

But Thomas Aquinas did not accept even for a moment the hypothesis of Arab thinkers. He maintained that the Agent intellect is something found in the soul itself and that it is really distinct from the possible intellect. But the activity of both is found in the soul itself and properly belongs to man. He criticised in his work *On the Unity of Intellect against the Averroists,* that if both the Active and Potential intellectual principles were numerically one in all men, we could not properly say that 'John thinks' or that 'William thinks'. We should have to say that 'it' (the intellect of the species or race) thinks in both men. Further, the theory of unity of the intellect cannot account for the obvious empirical fact that John and William can think differently and have different ideas and convictions.[3]

In order to make plausible that the Active intellect is a part of the individual soul, the views of Aquinas can be illustrated as follows:

1. If the Active intellect is not a part of the individual, knowledge could not strictly be attributed to the individual.
2. If the Agent intellect is outside the individual soul, there would be something difficient in the human soul.
3. The product of the Active intellect, like the product of possible intellect is attributed to the individual.

The debater about the unity of the Active intellect between Thomistic philosophers and Averroists no doubt had theological and metaphysical interests but for our purpose the theological significance or implications of the doctrine are not important. If we look at the debate purely from the perspective of epistemological analysis we can conclude that St. Thomas's doctrine of the Active intellect stresses the importance of some kind of activity as being a necessary condition of the possibility of human experience and knowledge. This point is of course put in theological terms as the necessary presence of the Active intellect as integral to the human soul which knows; in his terms it is not outside the human soul but a necessary element of the soul which makes it possible to have knowledge. The idea of knowledge as presupposing an active synthesis may be taken as an anticipation of one of the central doctrines of the Critical Philosophy of Kant. Understood in this manner, the Medieval debate about the Active intellect has a surprising relevance for our problem.

REFERENCES

1. J. H. Randall, *The Career of Philosophy*, Vol. I (Columbia University Press, New York and London: 1966) p. 28 Note.
2. *De Anima*, III, 5, Trans; Foster and Humphries (New Heaven, Yale University, 1954) pp. 425-26.
3. Cf., F. C. Copleston, *A History of Medieval Philosophy*, (Metheun & Co. Ltd. 1972) p. 122.

APPENDIX B

A NOTE ON LOCKE'S POLEMIC CONCERNING INNATE IDEAS

There has been a considerable discussion on, who were the oponents Locke had chiefly in mind concerning the polemic of innate ideas. The only writer Locke refers by name is Lord Herbert of Cherbury,[1] but as he had not heard of Lord Herbert of Cherbury's book till his own argument was fully under way, he must have had others in view when he undertook the controversy.

It has been generally supposed that Locke's polemic was directed against the Cartesians, because in Descartes' philosophy, the doctrine of innate ideas occupied a very prominant place. Descartes' chief argument for the existence of God is the innateness of the ideas of a perfect being. Locke refers to this argument. when he is dealing himself with the existence of God in Book IV of the *Essay* and Prof. Gibson points out the repreated use in Book I of the *Essay* of Descartes' term "*adventitious*" *as* opposed to "innate",[2] shows that the Cartesian doctrine was present to his mind when he wrote the *Essays.* But from the form of the argument which Locke's polemic assumes, clearly shows that it was not the Cartesian position which he had primarily in view. In Locke's case the argument is throughout against 'innate-principles' and only secondarily or inferentially against 'innate ideas'. Therefore, Prof. Gibson argues that Locke's statement, that if the upholders of "*innate principles*", had but realised that the innateness of a proposition implies the innateness of the ideas which make it up, "they would not perhaps have been so forward to believe" in the doctrine of innate truths or principles. This remark by itself, Prof. Gibson adds is sufficient to refute the supposition that the polemic is primarily directed against the Cartesians.[3] Moreover the appeal to the *Universal Consent* which Locke associates so prominently with the doctrine he is attacking forms no part of the theory of innate ideas as we find it in Descartes. Therefore Prof. Gibson has clearly shown that Locke's real antagonists were the *Scholastic men*,[4] whose theory of reasoning from *maxims* he attacks in Seventh Chapter of Book IV of the *Essay*. The *magnified* maxims which he denies in Book IV to be, "the foundations of all our other knowledge", "the principles from which we deduce all other truths" are the same principles whose innateness he denies in Book I of the *Essay*. He takes the same instances, whose magnified principles of demonstration, '*Whatever is, is*' and '*It is impossible for the samething to be and not to be*' and the line of argument is in both cases same. It is clearly evident from the above line of argument that Descartes was not the direct victim of the polemic, rather as suggested by Gibson, they were the university teachers of his day.[5] Taking this view of Gibson, Aaron answered, "but I hardly suppose that Prof. Gibson wishes us to believe that the attack was meant solely for them."[6]

F.C. Fraser confessed to the difficulty of finding the target of polemic.[7] Regarding Descartes being the target of the polemic, he writes: "But by an innate idea Descartes means something antecedent to all experience, potential in the constitution of the understanding, and not necessarily in consciousness—argued on the ground that the individual ideas contingently given in experience cannot fully explain ideas that are universal. This means, that the mind has an *innate faculty* for universal ideas."[8] He continued further that "only this sort of innateness was intended, Descartes expressly says, in explaining his meaning to Regius, who had insisted that innateness of ideas was not needed to solve the phenomena, innateness of faculty being enough. As to which Descartes says—Regius appears to differ from me merely in words; for when he says that the mind has no need of ideas that are innate, and meantime grants that we all have an innate faculty for thinking them, he asserts, in effect, what I myself hold, although he rejects it in words. For *I have never said or thought that the mind has ideas that are innate, in any other sense than that it has a faculty for thinking such ideas.*"[9] From the above it becomes clear that Descartes tried much to remove all absurdities from the *innateness doctrine* and the doctrine has been reduced to a meaning that would be acceptable to Locke.

Various writings reveal that the possible target of the polemic were the Cambridge Platonists. Because in the early part of the century of Hobbes and Locke, the influence of the Platonic revival was powerfully felt in Oxford and Cambridge. Cudworth, the pioneer of the Cambridge Platonic tradition, who propounded a theory of knowledge which was essentially Platonic, might be the Lockean target. Therefore, Cassirer taking the Cambridge School as the target of the polemic writes:

> In their defence of the *a priori*, most of the thinkers of the Cambridge School do not distinguish between the 'logical' and the 'temporal' sense of the *a priori* concept. Hence they argue not only for the *a priori* validity of theoretical and ethical principles, but also for the 'innateness' of those principles. In this respect they advocate essentially the position which Locke assails in the Book I of his *Essay*. And it is quite probable that Locke, in formulating his arguments, was aiming largely at the philosophers of Cambridge as his real oponents.[10]

The difficulty in tracing out the target of the polemic had become so acute, that it has been seriously suggested by some writers that Locke, in order to make his own views clearer, began by setting up a man of straw, presenting in a concrete and vivid fashion a theory of knowledge which no philosopher had ever actually upheld, and refuting it convincingly."[11] The above suggestion has been subsequently noticed by Aaron, which irked him to comment that "The reference to 'these men of innate principles' in the text are of such a kind that they seem to me to rule out the hypothesis. Moreover, Locke was not the man to waste powder and shot on imaginary opponents."[12] Even Woozley agrees that he is not attacking men of straw, but he cites only the old guesses of Descartes, Cudworth, and Lord Herbert of Cherbury.[13]

Taking this dispute to notice Copleston remarked that "His

(Locke) remarks about this theory being 'an established opinion amongst someman' and about their being 'nothing more commonly taken for granted' suggests perhaps that he was simply writing in general against the theory, without intending to direct his criticism against any individual in particular, Descartes, for example, or against a particular group, such as the Cambridge Platonists. He includes in a global fashion all the upholders of the theory."[14]

The above observations reveal that the target of the polemic has become very much controversial. Even Peter Gay in 1964—wrote that "the precise target of his long polemic remains a matter of discussion."[15]

REFERENCES

1. A. C. Fraser, *Essay Concerning Human Understanding*, Dover Publications, 1959, vol. I and II, Book II ch. ii, 15. p. 80.
2. James Gibson, *Locke's Theory of Knowledge and its Historical Relations*, Cambridge, 1968. p. 43.
3. Ibid., p. 230.
4. Ibid., p. 42.
5. Ibid., p. 41.
6. Aaron, *John Locke*, Oxford, 1955. p. 89.
7. Essay, p. xxi.
8. Ibid., p. xxi-xxii.
9. Ibid., p. xxii (Halics are mine).
10. Cassierer, *Platonic Renaissance in England*, trans. Pettogrove, Nelson, 1953, p. 59 Note.
11. For instance, Cassirer, *Das Erkenntnis*, ii. 230-1, Leans to this view (Cf. *John Locke*, Aaron. p. 89).
12. Aaron, *John Locke*, p. 89.
13. A. D. Woozley, *An Essay C. H. U.*, Fontana, 1975 pp. 16-17.
14. Copleston, *A History of Philosophy*, Vol. V p. 74.
15. Peter Gay, *John Locke on Education*. p. 7. (Cf. *Locke and The Compass of H. U.*, J. W. Yolton, Cambridge, 1970. p. 173 Note).

APPENDIX C

A NOTE ON LEIBNIZ AND LOCKE ON INNATE-IDEAS

My main concern in this note would be to see how Leibniz reacted to the polemic of Locke on innate-ideas and his own limitations. While discussing I would refer primarily to Leibniz's *Nouveaux Essais.*[1]

When Leibniz found himself at variance with Locke on psychological and epistemological issues, he wrote his NE concerning human understanding. This treatise was completed in 1704, the year of Locke's death, but did not appear until 1765, when Lockean empiricism had already run its course of development.

Locke after denying the existence of innate-principles and ideas in the 1st Book of the *Essay Concerning Human Understanding,* begins the second by comparing the mind to "white paper void of all characters". More precisely he held that the mind which is concerned with ideas and knowledge is empty at birth and that is filled up through the channels of sensation and reflection.

Leibniz reacted to the above metaphor used by Locke, and claimed that it is inadequate and presented his own[2] where he has suggested that innate truths and ideas exist ready formed in the mind and need only to be brought to light. Taking all the views into consideration, Leibniz reacted against Locke in his NE, which reads—"Our differences are upon subjects of some importance. The question is to know whether the soul in itself is entirely empty as the tablets upon which as yet nothing has been written (*Tabula-rasa*) according to Aristotle, and the author of the *Essay*, and whether all that is traced thereon comes solely from the senses and from experience; or whether the soul contains originally the principles of many ideas and doctrines which external objects merely call up on occasion."[3]

Leibniz reacted to the *tubula-rasa* doctrine of Locke and the mind being empty at birth but suggested that ideas and truths are for us innate, as inclinations, dispositions, habits or natural potentialities. Leibniz agreed with empiricists criticism of the doctrine of innate-ideas, that the mind does not started with any inborn explicit formulated principles. But suggested further that this never implies that the mind is initially blank. To Leibniz, mind is in its nature a thinking activity and this activity finds in the process of experience its characteristic manifestations in specific ideas. Leibniz claimed that there are no specific innate-ideas but the capacity to entertain ideas is what makes the mind a mind and this capacity of the mind cannot be imparted to it from without. Therefore to Leibniz the doctrine of *tabula-rasa*, that the mind being empty at birth has to be rejected.[4]

Leibniz defined his position very clearly by revising a famous scholastic formula that, "Nothing is in the understanding which was not previously in the sense." To this version of Locke, he added "except understanding itself (nisi ipse intellectus)[5] where Leibniz has maintained that unacquired and fundamentally characteristic power of intelligence in the mind. A development of this idea we would see in Kant's theory of knowledge.

Regarding the universal consent of innate-principles, which was the target of Locke, Leibniz asserts that he does not pretend to hold that the certainty of innate-principles is founded on universal consent, rather it proceeds from within ourselves; provided one can give attention to the light which is born with us. Leibniz claimed that there can be something in our mind of which the mind is not necessarily conscious. Therefore Leibniz carefully points out, that innate knowledge need not be actual (conscious), in most cases innate-knowledge is virtual. It is not actually thought about untill we give attention, even some of this knowledge will never be thought about (became conscious) at all. For Leibniz, we are not conscious in such cases, because the confused perceptions of the senses divert our attention from them and prevent the interior light from shining. And this notion of virtuality is the core of "except understanding itself", which Leibniz added to the official doctrine of Locke. Leibniz's reply would be that by saying that there is nothing in us of which we have not atleast formerly been conscious is to limit the thesis.[6]

Leibniz held that there is a basic distinction between the way we know necessary and universal truths, emerging from souls intellect and the way we know contingent and particular truths, emerging from the soul's sensibility. Therefore from a psychological and exoteric point of view, as expounded in NE, the first kind of truth may be called innate while the second may be called acquired. This clear identification of both necessary and contingent truth and the sources from which they are derived, is certainly a development Leibniz has attempted in order to defend his doctrine of innate ideas. I have already pointed out how Locke was put into a philosophical crisis by rejecting innate-ideas and accepting necessary truths. Because Locke while rejecting the innatism doctrine did not pretend to assume that universal and necessary knowledge could proceed from senses or that such knowledge was impossible at all. Locke restricted the necessary and universal knowledge to a very narrow field but they proceed from the understanding and goes beyond the senses. For Leibniz that never created a problem because he admits both innate and acquired knowledge. He does not deny the role of experience in the knowing process leading to innate truths. He is ready to admit that consciousness of innate truths is stimulated by sensation of external objects as 'Occasions'. But he made himself clear by suggesting that this does not mean they are derived from sensation. Because the senses can provide us with examples, i.e., individual or particular truths only, and these examples were not sufficient to establish the universal necessity of a truth. Therefore, truths relating to mathematics and geometry, to logic, metaphysics and ethics cannot be derived from the senses, they can be proved only through innate principles. They are pure ideas, necessary truths, primitive-innate-knowledge. They and their truths derived can be proved only by the understanding alone. If this is so, immediately we are facing a major point, how to reconcile the metaphysical doctrine that all ideas derive from the soul with the psychological doctrine of their double origin? Leibniz solved that very elegantly. He considers innate those ideas which are immediately distinct as soon as we became aware of them, they proceed from the understanding, i.e., they only need the light of nature to be verified, but knowledge which first appears in a confused way is considered to proceed from senses. In other words, Leibniz suggests that all ideas proceed from within our soul but the cognitive quality with which they are endowed provides a distinction between those we call innate and those we call empirical. While explaining his own views on the above issue, Leibniz also became very much critical of Locke's acceptance of reflection. Leibniz argued that, having employed the whole of 1st Book of *Essay* in rejecting innate-intelligence taken in a certain sense, Locke, nevertheless at the beginning of the Second Book, admits that the ideas which do not originate in sensation come from reflection. Leibniz claimed that reflection is nothing else than attention to what is in us and the senses do not give us what we already carry with us. Therefore Leibniz writes—"I am led to believe that at bottom his opinion upon this point is not different from mine, or rather from the common view, in as much as he recognises two sources of own knowledge, the senses and reflection"[7]

The above observations reveal that the reactions of Leibniz to the controversy on innate-ideas proved to be justifiable, inspite of the sound defence of the doctrine of innate-ideas, it could not be received well because the early eighteenth century philosophical atmosphere was certainly not favourable to innatism, which had decreased in Britain and was only supported in France only by some belated followers of Descartes and Malebranche. If the reactions after the publication of NE would be taken into consideration particularly English reaction in the Monthly Review,[8] we would find Leibniz's version or better misrepresentation of Locke's doctrine of the *tabula-rasa* is expounded without immediate criticism. But Leibniz's doctrine is clearly misrepresented by the Reviewer. Leibniz's distinction between necessary and contingent truth is simply overlooked. The English Reviewer missed the main point and ironic effort is infact nothing but an apology for Lockeanism.

Leibniz's analysis of necessary truths deduced from innate-principles and not from sensible induction, our soul contains the seeds of some ideas, the *tabula-rasa* doctrine has to be rejected, these lines were either overlooked or in most cases probably explained away as a version of Leibniz's metaphysical cognitive doctrine. Otherwise given a right interpretation, his doctrines might have emerged as a strong defence of innatism. Because Locke is assumed to reject any disposition or virtuality and not to admit the subsistance of anything in the understanding except actually conscious knowledge helped Leibniz to prove that this doctrine is untenable and to assert firmly the presence of innate-ideas.

Taking all the above views into consideration, now we can able to see whether Leibniz successfully met the polemic of innate-ideas or left some relevant philosophical issues relating to that unsolved.

1. Replying to the official doctrine of Locke, that "Nothing is in the understanding which was not previously in the sense" Leibniz added "except understanding itself." Here Leibniz did not explicitly mention what is that understanding or intellect? What are various levels of the intellect? Moreover he did not try to establish any theory of the understanding itself. This has been carried on by Kant subsequently in his *Critique of Pure Reason*, where he has contributed sufficiently to the analysis of human faculties and developed a sound theory of the intellect or understanding.

2. The theory of knowledge propounded by Leibniz reveals that, he does not give a proper account of experience in the formation of knowledge. Like Plato, he admits that experience serves as an occasion and stimulates innate-truths. Even though he has relegated the role of experience to a secondary importance—like Descartes in epistemology, his venture in this connection was not completely successful.

3. The question of necessary truth which has emerged as very much central in the polemic of innate-ideas, has not been given a final solution by Leibniz. The concept of necessary truth precisely put Locke into a very inconvenient position concerning his own official doctrine. In Leibniz, that concept also played a very prominent role in order to defend the innatism doctrine. To Leibniz human beings are capable of acquiring

propositional knowledge including knowledge of general truths; and we know some of this knowledge to be certain and this certainty is not derivable from observation and experience that only gives us inductive generalisations. Both observations of Leibniz here are correct; but neither of these gives any support to the claim that necessary truths are innate.

4. Leibniz while dealing with the polemic, merely takes of innate capacities or dispositions, without referring to the meaning of disposition and to verious forms of capacities. In NE, he has not given any account of how we acquire innate-ideas, rather the emphasis is on how are they extracted. This failure in a clear conception of dispositions and its activities put Leibniz in a difficult situation, so that he could not clearly answer what kind of judgment could said to be necessary and innate?

To sum up the achievements of Leibniz, we could see that inspite of the poor responce his NE received, it nevertheless prompted Kant to refuse to accept empiricism as a satisfactory philosophy.[9] The strength of Leibniz's theory of knowledge lies in the acceptance of two sources of knowledge those that are innate and those that are acquired or necessary and contingent respectively. Before Leibniz both Descartes and Locke were having their extreme views, i.e. that either reason or experience respectively, besides their loose acceptance to the other non-officially. Therefore Leibniz is rightly praised for his doctrine of the origin of knowledge as a very reasonable compromise between Descartes and Locke.[10]

REFERENCES

1. My reference would be to the Translation of *Nonveaux Essais* by A. G. Langley—London, The Open Court Publishing Co., 1916. Here after I will mention only (NE).
2. Ibid., 45-46 pp.
3. Ibid., p. 42.
4. Erdmann, TR, p. 446
5. NE, Langley p. 111.
6. Ibid. p. 46.
7. Op. cit., NE, A. G. Langley, p. 47.

8. Monthly Review-XXXIII (1765) 497 ff. For reactions of N. E. in Germany and France please see details in *Journal of History of philosophy*, October 1974—"Leibniz on Innate-ideas and early reactions to the publication of NE (1765)" by Giorgio Tonells.
9. Weldon, *Kant's Critique of Pure Reason*, p. 58, Oxford, 1958.
10. J. G. Buhle—(Geschichte der Philosophie IV) (Gottingen 1803) the greatest historian of his day, referred to the NE (pp-127-275 ff) while expounding Leibniz's system. (Cf. *Journal of History of Philosophy* "Leibniz on Innate-ideas and the Early reactions to the publication of NE (1765)" by Giorgio Tonelli. October 1974).

Bibliography

Aaron, R.I., *John Locke*, Oxford, 1955.

——. *Knowing and the Function of Reason*, Oxford, 1971.

Allen, R.E., *Studies in Plato's Metaphysics*, Routledge & Kegan Paul, London, 1965.

Aristotle, *De Anima*, In the version of William of Moerbeke and the Commentary of St. Thomas Aquinas, translated by Foster, O. P., and Others, New Haven, Yale University, 1954.

Armstrong, A.H., *The Cambridge History of Later Greek and Early Medieval Philosophy*, Cambridge, 1967.

Austin, J. L., *Sense and Sensibilia*, Oxford, 1962.

——. *Philosophical Papers*, Oxford, 1970.

Ayer, A. J., *Logical Positivism* (ed.), Free Press, 1959.

——. *The Revolution in Philosophy*, Macmillan, 1970.

Beck, L. W., *Studies in the Philosophy of Kant*, Bobbs-Merrill, Company, Inc., 1965.

Bennett Jonathan, *Kant's Analytic*, Cambridge University Press, 1968.

——. *Kant's Dialectic*, Cambridge University Press, 1974.

Bergmann, Gustav., *Logic and Reality*, University of Wisconsin Press, Medison, 1964.

——. Bird, Graham, *Philosophical Tasks*, Hutchinson University Library, London, 1972.

———. Bluck, R. S., *Plato's Phaedo* (Translated with an introduction, notes and appendices), Routledge & Kegan Paul, London, 1955.

———. *Plato's Meno* (ed., with an introduction and commentary), Cambridge University Press, 1961.

Brehier, Emile, *The History of Philosophy: The Middle Ages and the Renaissance*, translated by Wade Baskin, the University of Chicago Press, 1968.

Broad, C. D., *Leibniz: An Introduction*, Cambridge University Press, 1975.

Broadie, Frederick., *An Approach to Descartes Meditations*, University of London, the Anthione Press, 1970

Buchdahl, Gerd., *Metaphysics and the Philosophy of Science* (the classical origins Descartes to Kant), Basil Blackwell, Oxford, 1969.

Burtt, E. A., *The Metaphysical Foundations of Modern Science*, Doableday, Anchor, 1932.

Carnap, Rudolf, *Logical Foundations of Probability*, London, Routledge & Kegan Paul, 1951.

Carus, Paul. (ed.), *Kant's Prolegomena to any Future Metaphysics*, The Open Court Publishing Co., 1949.

Cassirer, E., *The Philosophy of Symbolic Forms*, Vols. I & II, translated by, Ralph Maniheim, New Haven, Yale University Press, 1957.

———. *The Platonic Renaissance in England*, translated by, James P. Pettingrove, Nelson, 1953.

———. *The Philosophy of the Enlightment*, translated by Fritz C.A. Koelln & J. P. Pettegrove, Beacon Press, Boston, 1955.

———. *The Individual and the Cosmas in Renaissance Philosophy*, translated by, M. Domandi, Oxford Basil Blackwall, 1963.

———. *The Problems of Knowledge* (Philosophy Science & History Since Hegel), translated by W. H. Woglem and C. W. Hendel, New Haven, Yale University, 1950.

Cassirer, E., Kristeller, O. P. and Randal, J. H., Jr. (ed.), *The*

Renaissance Philosophy of Man, Phoenix Books, University of Chicago Press, 1956.

Cassirer, H. W., *Kant's First Critique*, London, Allen & Unwin, 1954.

Chappell, V.C. (ed.), *Ordinary Language: Essays in Philosophical Method*, Prentice-Hall, Inc., 1964.

Chomsky, Noam, *Cartesian Linguistics*, New York, Harper & Row, 1966.

Collingwood, R. G., *An Essay on Philosophical Method*, Oxford, 1950.

Collins, James, *Interpreting Modern Philosophy*, Princeton University Press, 1972.

Copleston, F. C., *A History of Philosophy*, London, Vols. I to VI.

——, *Aquinas*, Penguin Books, 1970.

– —. *A History of Medieval Philosophy*, Mathuen & Co., Ltd., 1972.

Cornford, F. M., *Plato's Theory of Knowledge*, Routledge & Kegan Paul, London, 1960.

Cranston, Maurice, *John Locke A Biography*, Longmans, 1957.

Crombie, I. M., *An Examination of Plato's Doctrine*, Routlege & Kegan Paul, London, 1962-63.

——. *Plato, the Midwife's Apprentice*, Routledge & Kegan Paul, London, 1964.

Curtis, S. J., *A Short History of Western Philosophy in the Middle Ages*, Macdonald & Co., London, 1950.

Dampier, William Cecil, *A History of Science and its Relations with Philosophy and Religion*, Cambridge at the University Press, 1948.

De Vleeschauwer, H. J., *The Development of Kantian Thought*, The History of a doctrine translated by A. R. C., Duncan, Thomas Nelson and Sons Ltd., 1962.

Dijksterhuis, E. J., *The Mechanization of the World Picture*, Oxford, 1961.

Doney, Willis (ed.), *Descartes, A Collection of Critical Essays*, Modern Studies in Philosophy Series, Macmillan, 1968.

Dryer, D. P., *Kant's Solution for Verification in Metaphysics*, London, George Allen & Unwin, 1966.

Dummet, Michael, *Frege, Philosophy of Language*, Duckworth, 1973.

During and Owen (ed.), *Aristotle and Plato in Mid-fourth centnry*, Goteborg, 1960.

Engel, S. M., *Wittgenstein's Doctrine of the Tyranny of Language*, An historical and critical examination of his Blue Book, Martinus Nijhoff, The Hagul, 1971.

Farber, Marvin, *The Aims of Phenomenology* (The motives, methods and impact of Husserl's Thought), Cambridge, 1975.

——. (ed.), *Philosophical Essays in Memory of Edmund Husserl*, Greenword Press, 1968.

Ferm, Vergilius, (ed.), *A History of Philosophical Systems*, The Philosophical Library N. K., 1950.

Findlay, J. N., *Plato the Written and Unwritten Doctrines*, London, Routledge & Kegan Paul.

Flavell, J. H., *The Developmental Psychology of Jean Piaget*, D. Van Nostrand Co., Inc., 1963.

Flew, Antony, (ed.), *Essays in conceptual Analysis*, Macmillan, 1966.

Fraser, A. C., (ed.), *An Essay concerning Human Understanding*, 2 Vols. Dover Publications, Inc., New York, 1959.

Gibson, A. B., *The Philosophy of Descartes*, London, Methuen & Co., Ltd., 1932.

Gibson, James, *Locke's Theory of Knowledge and its Historical Relations*, Cambridge, 1931.

Gilson, F., *History of Christian Philosophy in the Middle Ages*, Sheed and Ward, London, 1955.

——. *The Christian Philosophy of St. Augustine*, Victor Gollanex Ltd., London, 1961.

——. *The Christian Philosophy of St. Thomas Aquinas*, Victor Gollancz, Ltd., London, 1961.

Graham, Keith, *J. L. Austin, A Critique of Ordinary Langnage Philosophy*, The Harvester Press, 1977.

Gulley, Norman, *Plato Theory of Knowledge*, London, 1962.

Habermas, J., *Knowledge and Human Interests*, translated by J. J. Shapiro Heinemann, London, 1972.

Hall, A., Rupert, (ed.), *The Making of Modern Science*, Leicester University Press, 1960.

Hamlyn, D.W., *Sensation and Perception*, (A History of the Philosophy of perception), New York, The Humanities Press, 1961.

Hartnack, Justus, *Kant's Theory of Knowledge*, Translated by Hartshorne, M. H., Macmillan, 1968.

Herbert, Feigl, Sellars, and Lehre, (ed.), *New Readings in Philosophical Analysis*, Meredith Corporation, 1972.

Hick, John, *Faith and Knowledge*, Cornell University Press, 1966.

Hook, Sidney, (ed.), *Language and Philosophy, A Symposium*, N.Y. University Press, 1969.

Hospers, John, *Readings in Introductory Philosophical Analysis*, Prentice-Hall, 1968.

Husserl, Edmund, *Ideas, General Introduction to Pure Phenomenology*, Translated by W. R. Boyce Gibson, New York, Coller Books, 1962.

——. *Logical Investigations*, Vols. I & II, Translated by J. N. Findlay, London, Routledge & Kegan Paul, 1970.

Jaeger, W., *Aristole-Fundamentals of the History of his Philosophy*, Oxford University Press, 1962.

Joachim, H. H., *Descartes Rules for the Direction of the mind*, ed., by Errlo E. Harris, London, George Allen & Unwin, Ltd., 1957.

Keeling, S. V., *Descartes*, Oxford, 1968.

Kemp, John., *The Philosophy of Kant*, Oxford University Press, 1968.

Kenny, Anthony (ed.), *Aquinas*, Modern Studies in Philosophy Series, Macmillan, 1970.

Knowles, David, *The Evolution of Medieval Thought*, Longman, 1970.

Korner, S., *Fundamental Questions of Philosophy*, Penguin Books, 1973.

——. *Kant*, Penguin Books, 1977.

Kristeller, P. O., *Renaissance Thought. The Classic Scholastic and Humanistic Strains*, Harper & Brothers, N.Y., 1961.

——. *Renassiance Thought II, Papers, on Humanist and the Arts*, Harper Torch Books, 1965.

——. *Eight Philosophers, of the Italian Renaissance*, Stanford University Press, 1966.

Lamprecht, S.P., *Our Philosophical Traditions (A brief History of Philosophy in Western Civilisation)*, New York, 1955.

Leibniz, G.W., Von., *New Essays Concerning Human Understanding*, Translated and ed., by A. G. Langley, the Open Court Publishing Co., Chicago, London, 1916.

Lindsay, A. D., *Kant*, Oxford University Press, 1936.

Mabbott, J. D., *John Locke*, Macmillan, 1963

Mackie, J. L., *Problems from Locke*, Oxford, 1976.

Mandelbaum, Maurice, *Philosophy, Science* and *Sense-perception*, Baltimore, 1964.

Maritain, Jacques, *Distinguish to Unite or the Degrees of Knowledge*, Translated by Gerals B. Phelan, Geoffrey Bles, London, 1959.

Martin, C. B. & Armstrong, (ed.), *Locke & Berkeley*, Modern Studies in Philosophy Series, Macmillan, New York, 1968.

Martin, Gottfried, *Leibniz Logic and Metaphysics*, Translated by Northcott & Lucas Manchester University Press, 1960.

Mathews, G., *Plato's Epistemology and Related Logical Problems*, Faber & Faber, London, 1972.

Maurice de Wulf, *History of Medieval Philosophy*, Vol. I, Translated by E. C. Messenger, Thomas Nelson & Sons Ltd., 1952.

McKeon, Richard, (ed.), *The Basic Works of Aristotle*, Randon House, N. Y., 1941.

Mischel, Theodore, (ed.), *Cognitive Development and Epistemology*, Academic Press, 1971.

Moore, G. E., *Philosophical Papers*, George Allen & Unwin, 1959.

Morris, C. R., *Locke, Berkeley*, Hume, Oxford, 1931.

Mourant, J. A., *Introduction to the Philosophy of St. Augustine*, the Pennsylvania State University Press, 1964.

Muirhead, John, H., *The Platonic Tradition in Anglo-Sexon Philosophy*, George Allen & Unwin, 1931.

Mundle, C. W. K., *A Critique of Linguistic Philosophy*, Clarendon Press, Oxford, 1970.

Oates, W. J., (ed.), *Basic Writings of St. Augustine*, Vol. I & II, Random House Publishers, N. Y., 1948.

O' Connor, D. J., *John Locke*, Pelican Books, 1952.

——. *New Studies in Ethics, Aquinas and Natural Law*, Macmillan, 1967.

O'Neil. *On Critical Theory*, New York, 1976.

Pap, Arther, *Semanties and Necessary Truth: An Inquiry into Foundations of Analytic Philosophy*. New Haven, Yale University Press, 1958.

Parkinson, G. H. R., *Leibniz Philosophical Writings*, Translated by Mary Morris & G. H. R. Parkinson, J. M. Dent & Sons Ltd., London, 1973.

Passmore, John, *The Philosophical Reasoning*, Gerald-Duckworth & Co., 1961.

——. *A Hundred years of Philosophy*, Penguin Books, 1975.

Paton, H. J., *Kant's Metaphysics of Experience*, Vols. I & II, London, Allen & Unwin, 1961.

Pears, David, *Wittgenstein*, Fontana, 1971.

Pegis, A. C., (ed.), *Introduction to St. Thomas Aquinas*, The Modern Library, New York, 1948.

Piaget, Jean, *Structuralism*, Translated by, Maschler, C., London, Routledge & Kegan Paul, 1971.

——. *The Mechanisms of Perception*, Translated by G. N. Seagrim, London, Routledge & Kegan Paul, 1969.

——. *The Origin of Intelligence in the Child*, Translated by Cook, M. London, Routledge & Kegan Paul, 1953.

——. *Genetic Epistemology*, Translated by Duckworth, E., Columbia University Press, 1970,

——. *Psychology and Epistemology, Towards a Theory of Knowledge*, Ttranslated by, P. A. Wells, Penguin Books, 1972.

——. *Insights & Illusions of Philosophy*, Translated by Wolfe Mays, London, Routledge & Kegan Paul, 1971.

——. *The Principles of Genetic Epistemology*, Translated by Wolfe Mays London, Routledge & Kegan Paul, 1972.

Pivcevic, Edo, *Husserl and Phenomenology*, Hutchinson, University Library, London, 1970.

——. (ed.) *Phenomenology and Philosophical Understanding*, Cambridge, 1975.

Prosch, Harry, *The Genesis of Twentieth Century Philosophy*, George Allen & Unwin, 1966.

Quine, W. V. O., *Word and Object*, The Technology Press of M.I.T., 1960.

——. *Selected Logic Papers*, Random House, N.Y., 1966.

Randal, J. H., Jr., *The Making of the Modern Mind*, Houghton Mifflin Co., 1954.

Randal, J. H., *The Career of Philosophy from Middle Ages to the Enlightment*, Columbia University Press, London, 1966.

Reichenbach, Hans, *Modern Philosophy of Science*. Translated & ed., by Maria Reichenbach Routledge & Kegan Paul, New York, 1959.

Rene', Descartes, *A Discours on Method, etc.*, Translated by John Veitch. Everyman's Library, London, 1951.

——. *Descartes, Philosophical Writings*, Translated by Smith Norman Kemp, London, Macmillan & Co., Ltd., 1952.

——. *Descartes, Philosophical Writings*, Translated by Anscombe, E., and Peter Thomas Geach, Edinburgh, Thomas Nelson & Sons, Ltd., 1954.

——. *The Philosophical Works of Descartes*, Vol. I & II, translated by Haldane E. S., & Ross, G. R. T., Dover Publications, Inc., 1955.

Rorty, Richard, (ed.), *The Linguistic Turn*, (Recent Essays in Philosophical method), the University of Chicago Press, 1968.

Ross, W. D., *Plato's Theory of Ideas*, Clarendon Press, Oxford, 1951.

Roth, John, K., *Problems of the Philosophy of Religion*, Chandler Publishing Co., 1971.

Roth, Leon. *Descartes' Discourse on Method*, Oxford, 1937.

Russell, Bertand, *A Critical exposition of the Philosophy of Leibniz*, London, George Allen & Unwin, 1967.

Sayre, K.M., *Plato's Analytic Method*, University of Chicago Press, 1969.

Sesonske & Fleming, (ed.), *Plato's Meno: Text & Criticism* Wads-worth Publishing Co., Inc., 1968.

Shorey, Paul, *The Unity of Plato's Thought*, Chicago Press, 1960.

Smith, Norman, Kemp, *New Studies in the Philosophy of Descartes*; *Descartes as Pioneer*, London, Macmillan & Co. Ltd., 1852.

——. *A Commentary to Kant's Critique of Pure Reason*, Macmillan, London, 1930.

Solomon, R. C., (ed.), *Phenomenology and Existentialism*, Harper & Row, 1972.

Sorabji, Richard, *Aristotle on Memory*, Duckworth, 1972.

Sorley, W. R., *A History of British Philosophy to 1900*, Cambridge University Press, 1965.

Spiegelberg, H., *The Phenomenological Movement*, A Historical Introduction, Vol. I & II Martinus Nijhoff, The Hague, 1971.

Stigen, Anfinn, *The Structure of Aristotle's Thought, An Introduction to the study of Aristotle's Writings*, Humanities Press, N.Y., 1966.

Strawson, P. F., *Individuals, An Essay in Descriptive Metaphysics*, Mathuen & Co., London, 1959.

——. *The Bounds of Sense, An Essay on Kant's Critique of Pure Reason*, Mathuen & Co., Ltd., London, 1966.

——. *Freedom and Resentment and Other Essays*, Mathuen & Co., Ltd., 1974.

Swing, T. K., *Kant's Transcendental Logic*, Yale University Press, 1969.

Taylor, A. E., *Aristole on his Predecessors*, The Open Court Publishing Co., 1959.

Tipton, I. C., *Locke on Human Understanding*, (ed.), *Selected Essays*, Oxford, 1977.

Tsanoff, Radostav A., *The Great Philosophers*, Harper & Row, 1964.

Urban, W. M., *Beyond Realism and Idealism*, George Allen & Unwin, 1949.

Urmson, J. O., *Philosophical Analysis, Its Development between Two World Wars*, Oxford, 1969.

Vlastos, G., (ed.), *Plato, Modern Studies in Philosophy Series*, 1; Metaphysics & Epistemology, Anchor Books, 1971.

——. (ed.), *The Philosophy of Socrates, A Collection of Critical Essays*, Modern Studies in Philosophy Series. Anchor Books, 1971.

——. *Platonic Studies*, Princeton University Press, 1973.

Vonleyden, W., *Seventeenth Century Metaphysics*, An Examination of some main concepts & theories, Gerald Duckworth & Co., Ltd., 1971.

Walsh, W. H., *Kant's Criticism of Metaphysics*, At University Press, Edinburgh, 1975.

Warnock, G. J., *English Philosophy Since 1900*, Oxford, 1958.

Weldon, T. D., *Kant's Critique of Pure Reason*, Oxford, 1958.

Wiener, Philip P, (ed.), *The Roots of Scientific Thought*, A Cultural Prospective, Basic Books Publishers, N.Y., 1958.

Wightman, W. P. D., *Science & the Renaissance, An Introduction to the Study of the Emergence of the Sciences in the Sixteenth Century*, Oliver & Boyd, Great Britain, 1962.

Wilkerson, T. E., *Kant's Critique of Pure Reason*, Oxford, 1976.

Winch, Peter, (ed.), *Studies in the Philosophy of Wittgenstein*, London, Routledge & Kegan Paul, 1969.

Windelband, W., *A History of Philosophy*, the Macmillan Co., 1901.

Wippel, John, F. & Wolter, Allen B., *Medieval Philosophy, from St. Augustine to Nicholas of Cusa*, The Free Press, N.Y., 1969.

Wittgenstein, Ludwig, *Philosophical Investigations*, translated by G.E.M. Anscombe, New York, Macmillan, 1968.

——. *Tractatus Logico-Philosophicus*, translated by, D.F. Pears and B.F. McGuinness, N.Y., Humanities Press, 1961.

Wolf, R.P., (ed.), *Kant, A Collection of Critical Essays*, Modern Studies in Philosophy Series, Macmillan, 1968.

Wolfe , Mays, & Brown, S.C., (ed.), *Linguistic Analysis & Phenomenology*, Macmillan, 1972.

Woozley, A. D., *John Locke, An Essay Concerning Human Understanding, Fontana*, 1975.

Yotton, J. W., (ed.), *An Essay Concerning Human Uunderstanding*, 2 Vols. J.M. Dent & Sons Ltd., London, 1961.

——. *Locke & the Compass of Human Understanding* (A selective commenting on the Essay), Cambridge, 1970.

——. *John Locke & the Way of Ideas*. Oxford, 1959.

Zaner, R.M., *The Way of Phenomenology Criticism as a Philosophical discipline*, Pegasus, N.Y. 1970.

Selected Articles

Barlingay, S. S., "Distinguishables & Separables", *Indian Philosophical Quarterly*, 1975, Vol. II, No. 2, pp. 153-169.

Cob, William, S., Jr., "Anemnesis, Platonic doctrine or sophistic Absurdity?" *Dialogue*, 1973 Vol. XII, No. 4, pp. 604-628.

Donceel, J., "Transcendental Thomism" *Monist*, 1974, Vol. 58, No. 1, pp. 67-85.

Glouberman, M., "The Methodological Development of Critical Philosophy", *Journal of the History of Philosophy*, 1979, Vol. XVII, No. 32, pp. 217-242.

Greenlee, Douglas, "Locke & the controversy over Innate Ideas", *Journal of the History of Ideas*, 1972, 33.

Imlay, Robert, A., "Intuition & the Cartesian Circle", *Journal of the History of Philosophy*", 1973, Vol. XI, pp. 19-27.

Jolley, Nicholas, "Perception & Immortality in the Nouveaux Essays", *Journal of the History of Philosophy*, 1978, Vol. XVI, No. 2, pp. 181-194.

Kenneth, Dorter, "The Reciprocity & the Structure of Plato's Phaedo", *Journal of the History of Philosophy*, 1977, Vol. XI, No. 1, pp. 1-11.

Landgrebe, Ludwig, "The Phenomenological Concept of Experience", *Philosophy & Phenomenological Research*, 1973, Vol. XXXIV, No. 1, pp. 1-13.

McMullin, Eranan, "Medieval & Modern Science, Continuiety or Discontinuity", *International Philosophical Quarterly*, 1965, Vol. V, No. 1, pp. 103-129.

Morris, John, "Descartes' Natural Light", *Journal of the History of Philosophy*, 1973, Vol. XI, pp. 169-187.

Nathanson, S. L., "Locke's Theory of Ideas", *Journal of the History of Philosophy*, 1973, Vol. XI, pp. 29-42.

Odegard, Douglas, "Locke as an Empiricist", *Philosophy*, 1965, 40, pp. 185-96.

Rescher, M., "A Newlook at the Problem of Innate Ideas", *British Journal of Philosophy of Science*, 1966, Vol. 17, pp. 205-218.

Rotenstreich, Nathan, "An Analysis of Piaget's Concept of Structure", *Philosophy & Phenomenological Research*, 1977, Vol. XXXVII, pp. 368-380.

Savile, Antony, "Leibniz's Contribution to the theory of Innate-Ideas", *Philosophy*, 1972, Vol. XLVII, No. 180, pp. 113-124.

Schouls, Peter, A., "The Cartesian Method of Locke's Essay Concerning Human Understanding", *Canadian Journal of Philosophy*, 1975, Vol. IV, pp. 579-601.

Stout, A. K., "The Basis of Knowledge in Descartes", *Mind*, 1929, Vol. XXXVIII, No. 151, pp. 330-342, and No. 152, 1929, pp. 458-472.

Tonelli, Giorgia, "Leibniz on Innate-Ideas & the Early Reactions to the Publication of the Nouveaux Essais 1765", *Journal of the History of Philosophy*, 1974, Vol. XII, No. 4, pp. 437-454.

Wall, Grenville, "Locke's attack on Innate Knowledge" *Philosophy*, 1974, Vol. 49, No. 190, pp. 414-419.

Wright, J. N., "The Method of Descartes", *Philosophical Qurterly*, 1955, Vol. 18, pp. 78-82.

Yolton, J. W., "Locke & the Seventeenth Century Logic of Ideas", *Journal of the History of Ideas*, 1955, 16, pp. 431-52.

Index

K

L

M

N

O

P

Q

R

S

T

U

V

W

Y